CHAMELEON CHRISTIANITY

CHAMELEON CHRISTIANITY

MOVING BEYOND SAFETY AND CONFORMITY

DICK KEYES

Wipf and Stock Publishers
EUGENE, OREGON

Wipf and Stock Publishers
199 West 8th Avenue, Suite 3
Eugene, Oregon 97401

Chameleon Christianity
Moving Beyond Safety and Conformity
By Keyes, Dick
Copyright© January, 1999 Keyes, Dick
ISBN: 1-59244-151-3
Publication date: February, 2003
Previously published by Baker Books, January, 1999 .

To L'Abri students, past, present, and future, with gratitude for their help with these ideas and in hope that they might lead toward salt and light.

Contents

Part 1: The Polarization

1   The Power of Polarization   11

2   The Christian Chameleon   23

3   Tribal Life   39

Part 2: Pressure Points for Transformation

4   The Recovery of Apologetics   55

5   One Truth, One Way   71

6   The Church as Community   87

7   Returning to the Foundations   103

Appendix   115

Notes   119

Part 1

∞

The Polarization

1

⸿

The Power of Polarization

WE LIVE IN A TIME of moral confusion, division, and recrimina-
tion. Cries of crisis are so common that they are starting to put
people to sleep. As one diagnosis clashes against another, the
volume of the conversation is slowly rising.

What distinguishes our time is not necessarily greater evil
or immorality than before, but greater confusion about morality itself—despite widespread and passionate moral accusations
and the advent of ethics as a growth industry. Moral discussion
seems to be carried on with the tattered fragments of a system
of meaning long since abandoned.

WHAT GROUNDS FOR MORALITY?

As early as the 1920s, journalist Walter Lippmann pointed to a
profound change in the way Americans who "no longer believe
in the religion of their fathers" were thinking about right and
wrong. He wrote of the "dissolution of the ancestral order"[1] after
which people still had moral convictions and feelings, but had
lost confidence in their meaning. Were they just customs? Opinions? Biochemical activities in the brain? Or were they eternal
truths after all?

Lippmann wrote of his generation,

> . . . having lost faith, they have lost the certainty that their
> lives are significant, and that it matters what they do with

their lives. If they deal with young people they are likely to say that they know of no compelling reason which certifies the moral code they adhere to, and that, therefore, their own preferences, when tested by the ruthless curiosity of their children, seem to have no sure foundation of any kind. They are likely to point to the world around them and ask whether modern man possesses any criterion by which he can measure the value of his own desires, whether there is any standard he really believes in which permits him to put a term upon that pursuit of money, of power, and of excitement which has created so much of the turmoil and the squalor and the explosiveness of modern civilization."[2]

Since Lippmann's observations, national and international events have made these quandaries even more troubling. At such a time, it would seem that the Christian faith would be uniquely equipped to speak powerfully into our culture. After all, it provides the moral framework that modern secular culture so conspicuously lacks.

But regretfully, the Christian faith is not seen as a rallying point for those concerned for the moral state of our land. And people are not flocking to the doors of the church to discover a foundation for individual and collective life. For today's society is fundamentally apathetic about many issues that Christians consider most important.

Some topics, however, can still raise the blood pressure—think, for example, of feminism, homosexual rights, sex education, the environment, social freedom, racism, abortion, and the overarching virtue of being nonjudgmental. These are issues over which many of our neighbors hold deep convictions.

In each of these areas, however, evangelical Christians are not seen in places of moral leadership. On the contrary, evangelicals are perceived to be on the low moral ground. That is to say, many of our neighbors believe that regarding the issues they care most about, Christian people stand not on the side of good but solidly on the side of evil. Being confident that they have a higher moral ground than those who follow Jesus, they feel that they can afford to ignore his claims.

My purpose here is not to debate whose perception is true or false. That must be decided one issue at a time. Rather it is to point out that on many of the issues where our society is morally and emotionally involved, evangelical Christians are considered barbaric and bigoted. We are seen as part of the problem and not the solution.

Although this may not be a new state of affairs, the pressure is escalating noticeably. And, ironically, this perception is in stark contrast to evangelical Christians' own view of themselves as standing alone in the breach and holding back the country from moral anarchy.

Clearly there is a great discrepancy between these two pictures. In this book we will explore why this is so, looking at whether the church of Christ is doing things wrong, and if so how we can do better in the future.

MAKING WAVES FOR THE FATHER

Few biblical themes are more important as we struggle to respond to this situation than Jesus' teaching on being salt and light. He begins his Sermon on the Mount with the Beatitudes, describing characteristics of his followers. He ends his sermon with the double-Beatitude having to do with persecution.

Following this idea of hostility from the surrounding society, Jesus then introduces the images of salt and light:

> You are the salt of the earth; but if salt has lost its taste, how can its saltiness be restored? It is no longer good for anything, but is thrown out and trampled under foot.
>
> You are the light of the world. A city built on a hill cannot be hid. No one after lighting a lamp puts it under the bushel basket, but on the lampstand, and it gives light to all in the house. In the same way, let your light shine before others, so that they may see your good works and give glory to your Father in heaven (Matthew 5:13–16).

Jesus addresses not so much our individual moral character, but our interaction with society. Like rocks dropped into a pond, Christians are dropped into society. What kind of waves do they make? Jesus calls us to make waves that are positive and transforming while we simultaneously keep our distinctively Christian identity. This kind of living—being salt and light in our communities—will draw people to the Father.

As salt is to meat, so we are to preserve what is good in society while bringing out its life and flavor. Salt is not sugar and does not taste sweet, yet it improves the taste of the whole. So it is with God's people whose confrontation with the world may involve conflict but who leave the world a better place.

As light, we are to shine God's truth into all areas of life, pushing back the darkness. In the process we may give an uncomfortably honest diagnosis of the world's problems. As light we are also, by the way we live, to show something of God's purpose for what it is to be human, to point toward an ideal of Christ-likeness that is both realistic and beautiful.

THE POWER OF THE WORLD

Living as salt and light is much more difficult than we usually realize; Jesus, however, was not so naive about the sheer power of social forces. He warned us against aborting the mission and becoming saltless salt or hidden light.

Jesus was probably referring to the salt in the region of the Dead Sea, some of which was so diluted and contaminated by other chemicals that it still looked like salt but no longer worked or tasted like it. His hidden light image is more obvious—he refers to a light bright enough to illuminate a whole house being hidden under an opaque box. It may heat up the box but leaves the house in darkness.

Why do Christians fail to be salt and light? They fail because the world is a dangerous place, especially for those who are "out of line" with their society. Jesus says that we will be a dissonant group and will be ostracized if not persecuted. Saltless salt and hidden light describe two apparently safer ways to live. Each allows us to avoid rubbing shoulders with potential cynics or persecutors.

Sociologists tell us that dissonant groups within a larger society react to reduce the potential for friction in two predictable ways. One is to compromise their distinctive beliefs and way of life and so reduce their conflict with society. The other is to keep their dissonance and tribalize, retreating within their own group and thus losing contact with society. Intriguingly, this is exactly what Jesus was pointing to in these images, long before sociology was ever dreamed of.

CHAMELEON OR MUSK OX?

Saltless salt pictures the Christian blending in with the surrounding society just as a chameleon changes its color to blend in protectively with its surroundings. This is the Christian individual or group that adapts, accommodates, compromises, and is diluted. Like salt that has lost its taste, the Christian is useless to carry out Jesus' purposes because dissonance with the world has been reduced to resonance or sameness. A distinctive Christian identity is lost, and there is nothing to offer the world that the world does not already have.

The Christian chameleon disregards, rejects, or gradually loses interest in the theological ideas and ethical principles that jar against the accepted ideas of society, such as those concerning truth, sex, power, and money. The ideas that go first today are any that could suggest intolerance or claims of Christ's uniqueness. At the same time, the chameleon might affirm those Christian teachings that resonate with what society already believes.

Hidden light, in contrast, is Christian tribalism—the protective containment of Christian distinctiveness within the Christian ghetto or subculture. It entails Christian tribal dialects, tribal education, tribal music, tribal television, and even the Christian tribal yellow pages—all mystifying to those uniniti-

ated into the tribe. Much time is spent reassuring the member-
ship of the superiority of their beliefs and traditions over the terrible evils lying outside the fortress walls.

The psychology of tribal life demands proscribed answers
for most of life's questions. The New Testament, however, does
not give us enough of these rules to hold a tribe together; it
allows far too much freedom. So when a church or Christian
group becomes tribal, part of the process includes adding many
rules and prohibitions to the ethics of the New Testament. This
is especially true in a fast-changing society, where the church
would otherwise have to grapple constantly with new and complex issues from the outside world.

Evangelism becomes a particular problem for the tribal
church or group. Typically these people will not know others
socially who are not already Christians. Evangelism then
becomes artificial and contrived, if not insensitive and
belligerent.

If the pattern of saltless salt is the Christian as a chameleon,
hidden light is the Christian as a musk ox. Musk oxen are Arc-
tic animals that form a circle around the young or sick when in
danger from predators, with their horns facing outward. They
would illustrate Christian tribalism even better if they faced
inward, delivering the occasional blind kick with their hind legs
out in the direction of the threatening world.

A Christian group can so protect itself against contamination from the world that it loses contact with the world and
hides its light. It is a community in quarantine. Even bright light
covered by an opaque box is still darkness.

As with saltless salt, if light is hidden, intrinsic Christian
identity is lost. Jesus did not say, "Try to act like salt and light,"
he said you *are* salt and light; a city on a hill *cannot* be hidden. If
saltless salt points to the loss of Christian identity through assimilation with the world, hidden light shows the loss of identity
by locking up the truth away from the world.

WORLDLINESS THAT DIVIDES

The chameleon and the musk ox represent two opposite styles of worldliness. The chameleon blends in to become like the world, thus diminishing the danger of scorn or persecution. The musk ox is worldly too, but in a less obvious way: It roots its confidence more in the group's safe isolation and mutual affirmation than in God.

The tribe may see itself as spiritually elite, but actually it follows the pattern of any nonreligious minority group that stands out from the surrounding society. Tribalizing is what Vietnamese immigrants do in California; what Hasidic Jews do in New York; what most Americans do in non-European cultures. And tribalizing is exactly what some evangelical Christians are doing today.

Immigrant groups in America have traveled all the roads: Some have tribalized; others have assimilated; many have combined some variation of the two. There is nothing necessarily wrong when national or ethnic groups tribalize or assimilate into a wider culture. But it is wrong for Christians—as Christians—to tribalize, for Jesus calls us to set our identity in him and to be salt and light in the world.

I'm not trying to minimize the painful force of persecution as if Christians have only been self-protective in fearing trivial insults. At stake may be loss of job, influence, or safety as well as traumatic estrangement from others. These pressures can lead us to accommodate God's truth or to retreat farther behind the tribal wall. But Jesus calls us to have the courage not to take either escape route.

Both the compromising of the chameleon and the tribalizing of the musk ox limit the painful experience of being aliens and exiles in the world. Both remove the interface of relationships that could produce friction between Christian and non-Christian. And both derive primary security not from God but from human social comfort.

If I am a chameleon, I am so similar to those who are not Christians that I experience no conflicts over matters of faith. If I am a musk ox, I am so isolated from the world that I rarely make significant personal contact with those outside of my tribe. Under these two powerful social pressures, we are either disarmed by our compromise with the world or isolated in our attempts to protect ourselves from it. Our faith is therefore either privatized or marginalized. We have short-circuited Jesus' intention that we be in the world, but not of it.

Ironically, these two opposite responses of compromise and tribalism feed each other. One of the major incentives that drives Christians into tribalism is the fear of contamination and compromise. They look at the fast-changing world and see the dangers of accommodation in graphic detail. "Nothing is solid any more. People don't take a stand. What will the liberals concede next?"

They then look at those whom they see as compromisers and say to themselves, "Where can we find other Christians who will help us stand against the tide of relativism and moral passivity?" The tribal Christians' clarity and confidence seems to be the answer.

The other side of the ledger works just the same way. Christians look at those whom they see as tribal in their narrowness, isolation, and belligerence and say, "Help! This cannot be what the Christian faith is really like. I need to find some group that offers an alternative to this rigidity!" The only group or church they find may be one that has trimmed its theology and ethics to fit comfortably into the modern world.

This is the power of polarization. Each side produces specters that drive the other side further from truth and sanity. An example illustrates this dynamic:

Some years ago I received two letters in the same week. One was from the Moral Majority and the other was from Katharine Hepburn, writing for Planned Parenthood. The messages were almost exactly the same. Both could be paraphrased, "There is a well-funded and powerful minority in this country that is trying to take away all that America stands for, as well as your own personal freedom. But there is hope—we are here. Your contribution will help us stand against this group and the destructive legislation that they sponsor at this critical moment in our nation's history."

The rhetoric was identical although the political perspectives were violently opposed. Neither group made an argument but rather each fed off their followers' fear of the other.

EXAMPLES FROM THE BIBLE

Biblical history illustrates the three ways of handling the tensions that we have described. We can see the first, the predominant sin of the chameleon—assimilation and compromise—when the Israelites occupied the promised land under Joshua.

The people of God went against the terms of the covenant and the warnings of the prophets when they adopted the idolatries of the Canaanite people. They tried to have the best of both worlds by combining these unholy practices with worship of the Lord. But they were judged when in the sixth century God allowed the Babylonians to defeat them and deport them to Babylon.

The second sin is illustrated after the Jews returned from Babylon and began to lean in the direction of the musk ox. They were determined not to be chameleons again, as is reflected by the scant evidence of pagan idolatry in the cities they occupied. Tribalism, however, began to grow.

This tribalism flowered fully in the first century through the theology and ethics of the Pharisees. These leaders had hundreds of rules about Sabbath observance alone. When Jesus suggested that God had, could, and would work in the lives of those who were not Jewish, they tried to throw him off a cliff in his own home town.

The third option for handling the tension is the way that Jesus designed for the church to be in the world but not of it. To be salt and light is to defy the enormous social pressures either to compromise or to tribalize. It is to confound the predictions of those who would see the church necessarily polarized into saltless salt or hidden light.

The church is to be an oscillating body that comes together for sacraments, worship, prayer, teaching, and caring for each other. Then it is to go out into society and serve before coming back together again. Without compromising on the word of God, the church is also to reach to those outside in costly love and friendship.

One of my favorite examples of living as salt and light appears in the writing of the apostle Paul. He reminds the Thessalonians about his ministry when he was with them:

> . . . we speak, not to please mortals, but to please God who tests our hearts. As you know and as God is our witness, we never came with words of flattery or with a pretext for greed; nor did we seek praise from mortals, whether from you or from others, though we might have made demands as apostles of Christ. But we were gentle among you, like a nurse tenderly caring for her own children. So deeply do we care for you that we are determined to share with you not only the gospel of God but also our own selves, because you have become very dear to us (1 Thessalonians 2:4–8).

Two themes stand out here. First, Paul was uncompromising in his faithfulness to God's word, not trying to minimize conflict by flattery to elicit a more positive hearing. He was salty salt.

Second, there is no hint that his dissonance and refusal to compromise involved a tribal, belligerent attitude to those who were not believers. Indeed, he was gentle among them, as a nurse with a child. He lived not behind a fortress wall, but lovingly shared his life in their homes. We can easily imagine Paul staying up long nights as they experienced suffering and doubt or had struggles with their children. The light of the world was not hidden under a box, but, through Paul, was right there in their homes.

AVOIDING THE TWIN DANGERS

If the church fails to follow Jesus' teaching about salt and light, what will be the result? We will fail in our evangelism, in our life together, and in our attempt to influence society positively.

If we go in the direction of the chameleon we will fit nicely into the pattern of modernism, or old-style Enlightenment humanism. Following a flawed dream, we will believe that we can all work together and improve life on earth if only we would admit that our religious commitments are unimportant. We will then lose our dissonance and our ability to offer anything different from that of a secular society. We would become irrelevant and superfluous. In short, saltless salt.

But if we go in the direction of the musk ox we will unwittingly walk into the mold of postmodernism. A tribal church that is so enclosed in its own culture fulfills the postmodern, multicultural description of a society where each group is so isolated from the others that communication across cultural barriers is almost impossible. Differences overshadow commonality. The tribal church contributes to the rising spirit of fragmentation when each group's own "community of discourse" fuels separatism in race, class, sex, nationality, and ethnicity. The church that follows this direction will be marginalized—not just out of line with society but out of touch with it. In short, hidden light.

The polarizing forces that surround us are powerful—so much so that they can lead us into self-deception as we simultaneously become both a chameleon and a musk ox. Some of the most visible leaders of Christian tribalism (for example, the televangelists at their worst) have shamelessly blended in with the worst of the secular society's behavior in areas of sex, money, and fame. In other words, we can be saltless salt and hidden light at the same time in different areas of our lives.

At a theological level we have a powerful and vital answer to many of the problems of the modern world. But if we fail to be salt and light, we will betray our calling and become impotent because of the way we relate to the people around us. If we are affected by the polarizing forces that we have been describing, we will be pushed into relativism or rigidity.

Apologist Francis Schaeffer used to say that in our relationships with others it is relatively easy to show either the holiness of God or the love of God. It is quite easy to be either coldly uncompromising against sin or warmly tolerant of it. But what is difficult—and in fact impossible without the work of the Holy Spirit—is to show both God's holiness and love at the same time. When the two are together we are neither harsh nor bland.

We will look in the next chapters at an analysis of this polarization in the Bible and also in today's church. We will then consider two pressure points that could lead to transformation, the recovery of vital apologetics and the building of nontribal communities.

I will inevitably be speaking critically of various parts of the life of the church. I speak not as an outsider, but as one loyal to it. I have not given up on the church, but am convinced that it is a great source of hope. G. K. Chesterton once said that there is a pessimism that "whispers in a million ears that things are not good enough to be worth improving." He sought instead to remind people that "things must be loved first and improved afterwards. . . ."[3]

2

The Christian Chameleon

WE NOW TURN IN MORE DETAIL to the problem of the people of God being saltless salt, which I have described as the chameleon syndrome. What pressures can lead us to compromise and to sell our birthright? What motivates us to give in to these pressures or even to pursue them actively?

We will deal with two sources of tension: powerful ideas that can intimidate Christians and social forces that can lure Christians by seeming to offer the power to accomplish our goals quickly and efficiently. But first we will look at some of the motivations that draw people in the direction of the chameleon.

MOTIVATIONS GOOD, BAD, AND MIXED

Sometimes good motivations can lead us in bad directions. One such motivation comes from being afraid of and revolted by Christian tribalism. Some Christians see tribal rigidity, prejudice, inhumanity, self-righteousness, and the inability to tolerate differences or change and want no part of it. They see intentional isolation from those who are not Christians, and they know that is wrong. But where can they turn? Where are Christians with whom they can have commonness of mind, worship, and fellowship?

Often the only ones who seem to offer an alternative are those who have relaxed on biblical authority and who accept

23

almost any brand of theology and ethics. They affirm what is going on in the world, especially if it is new. And they seem less prejudiced and more open and kinder to their fellow creatures on earth.

This is one of the great dynamics of polarization. The person who is horrified at and perhaps wounded by Christian tribalism looks for an alternative, but it seems that the only one in sight is a church or group that has compromised seriously. Yet because it offers an alternative to tribalism, it looks much better than if viewed alone. The power of polarization drives people further in the opposite direction than they might have otherwise wanted to go. A sane middle ground becomes a lonely and radical place to stand.

A second motivation for compromise also starts as something positive—the notion that "all truth is God's truth," and so new ideas need not be feared. While this proposition is certainly true, it can also be expressed in a more dangerous way: "We can expose ourselves to anything and our faith will stand up to the challenge."

Although admirable for its courage, this conviction can be naive unless it is coupled with deep humility before God and an awareness of the destructive power of ideas and social influences. If we underestimate the power of these forces, we are likely to blend in with the ideas and ways of those living around us. No longer are we dissonant to them, but rather resonant with them.

This resonance is itself a third source of motivation, for we like to be liked. This is not necessarily bad, but it can lead us to avoid differing from those we are with to keep their approval. Being a chameleon can be the route to respectability, acceptance, and legitimacy in the eyes of those in the inner circles of power.[1]

Yet Jesus said, "Woe to you when all speak well of you, for that is what their ancestors did to the false prophets" (Luke 6:26). Accommodation can seem to offer peace and respectability, but Jesus says "woe to us" if we live to impress fools in high places.

A fourth motivation is the fear that God's truth will not stand up to scrutiny in the marketplace of ideas. This fear leads us to retreat to a more widely acceptable and therefore more easily defended position. It may be easy to back up far enough so that we avoid attack entirely.

What we face is a vast set of incentives working on us from the world of ideas as well as through the structures of society, encouraging us to accommodate. Let us look next at some important pressure points in ideas.

CHAMELEON IN IDEAS

Perhaps the most important point of all, because all else depends on it, is the pressure to compromise in our view of truth. Let me lay out some contours of the modern consensus about truth.

We are told that human beings cannot possibly know God or absolute truth. Anything we do know comes to us filtered and therefore distorted by our own self-deceptions, political agendas (known and unknown), and cultural limitations. This view is "religious relativism" because all that we think about God, including his existence, is understood as relative to and conditioned by our psychological profile, economic status, and cultural and historical peculiarities.

According to this outlook, we can hold opinions as private expressions of faith. These, however, are not seen to correspond to anything outside of the heads in which they are stored. They can be described as "true" only if what we mean is that they are truly helpful to the one who believes them sincerely.

And we can study human religious behavior in all its forms with the tools of psychology, demography, sociology, anthropology, and statistics. This knowledge can yield truths that do correspond to actual religious activities. But it gives us no understanding of God himself, just knowledge about what people believe and do who think they have found him, her, or it.

We live in an atmosphere that consists of these two levels of truth. One is public truth, such as truths about religious behavior, biochemistry, and political trends. In short, it is anything that the public can observe or check for its factuality.

The other level is truth about God and ultimate things. This is not public knowledge but rather private opinion or belief. It cannot be called true or false because it concerns a subjective set of preferences within each person, impossible for others to observe or contradict.

If we accept that truth is divided in this way, it leaves us with rigid restrictions on what knowledge is possible. It requires us to accept that no one can really know anything about God or ultimate truth.

The historic Christian claim that God has made himself known by revelation in words to ordinary human beings is seen as outrageous and impossible. It becomes worse still when it is understood that God has revealed that becoming reconciled to him only happens through Jesus Christ.

This exclusiveness of the claims of Christ is probably the biggest single offense today to people who do not see themselves as Christians—and to many who do. It draws hostility, condescension, and ridicule because it is radically dissonant to today's prevailing wisdom.[2]

THE BLOWING WINDS OF RELATIVISM

The pressure on the evangelical Christian from these ideas is increased by the social reality of pluralism. We live, work, and study next to people of other religions, philosophies, and world-views in a way that never happened even a hundred years ago. This change to a religiously more plural society does not make relativism true, but it may make it *seem* true.

Tolerance is rightly seen as a virtue. But today what is often implied by the word is *relativism*, thinly disguised under the positive connotations of the word *tolerance*. If you do not toe the line to relativism you are branded as intolerant, which is not tolerated. There is enormous pressure to conform.

If we have lost confidence that human knowledge about God can correspond to who God actually is, we are already bent to the wind of modern relativism. We will begin to see the Christian faith as a particularly Western European or North American version of a generic spirituality, one of many roads up the same mountain. We are likely to accept higher critical views of the Bible so that it no longer claims the authority of a unique verbal revelation of God. And we then see exclusive assertions that Jesus made about himself as only the imaginative reflections of the early church community who inflated his claims to comfort themselves after his death.

The pressure to accommodate is also powerful in the area of morality. If knowledge about God and ultimate reality is out of reach, then the absolute moral principles once rooted in God's authority must be unattainable as well. People in different cultures have different moral norms. No one culture can claim universality. Morality is relative to time and culture. There is no absolute good and bad, no right and wrong. Actions are *relatively* good or bad according to their context, motivation, and consequences.

The Christian who lives in the chameleon mode will bend to the currently respectable viewpoint on each ethical issue, whether abortion, sexual behavior, accumulation of wealth, or attitude toward other races. Into none of these issues will the Bible be allowed to speak authoritatively. Thus a saltless Christianity will always shape itself by taking from within Christian truth only those things that are socially resonant then and there. It will neglect or reject those Christian teachings that challenge the most respectable ideas of the culture.

Those who make all moral choices into black and white issues do reduce moral life to absurdity. But Christians who turn away from biblical moral absolutes altogether are also foolish. With no black or white there is only uniform, unbroken, medium gray. Without absolutes, relative good and evil is an illusion and a pretense, for they must be relative *to* something. No moral distinctions remain.

Christians who have lost a high view of truth take two routes in their journey of accommodation. One is to lose their dissonance reluctantly or perhaps so slowly that they do not realize what is happening.

The other is described as "aggressive accommodation" by sociologist James Hunter.[3] Often those who accommodate aggressively are people who have been profoundly hurt by Christian tribalism. They revel in ridiculing biblical faith and in championing the latest theological innovation or moral experimentation. Episcopal Bishop John Spong would be a good example today. He has shown that it is possible to understand the Christian faith as so resonant with the prevailing ideas of the culture that it is fully captive to it.

CHAMELEON TO SOCIAL PRESSURES

We now turn to the impact of the social forces we experience in these modern times, which bring different temptations than those we have been describing.

With the Industrial Revolution and all that has come with it, more and more of life is now covered by the systematic mastery of reality. Through the application of human techniques to life's contingencies we have developed skills and expertise (and accompanying experts) for every human activity—communication, management, personal growth, church growth, prayer, making love, and so on. Through our human technique we aim to break down all the variables of life into little pieces and then analyze, control, or fix them before putting them back together again.

The result is secularization. More and more of life's variables are controlled by human choice, intention, and action without reference to anything beyond human activity. God and the transcendent realm is made to seem irrelevant in those parts of life where the important things happen. Even those who believe in God have to pinch themselves to remember that he is behind all this technology and know-how, that it depends on him and does not run on its own.

For example, the late Henri Nouwen wrote of an experience while he was a chaplain on board a passenger ship. He was on the bridge in the midst of a thick fog as the captain was bringing the ship into harbor. The captain, nervously pacing around the bridge, bumped into Nouwen and cursed, telling him to keep out of the way. As Nouwen was retreating, filled with feelings of incompetence and uselessness, the captain relented and said, "Why don't you just stay around. This might be the only time I really need you."

For Nouwen the event illustrated Christian experience in the secularized modern world. Although we were once in the centers of power, we are now in the way. Our whole orientation to God and concern with him is seen to be obsolete, irrelevant, and superfluous in a technologically controlled world—except when a rare danger pushes us beyond what human technical competence can manage. Then our prayers might provide good luck or at least some comfort. The vast majority of "real life" goes on without reference to anything beyond the immediate cause-and-effect world that we seem to control.[4]

This modern view causes religious institutions to become marginalized. God's absence or irrelevance becomes more plausible than his presence and power, encouraging the retreat of faith from public life into private experience.

As a result, Christian leaders are not seen as major players in public life. Imagine what would happen to the status of physicians if, some day in the future, people determined that the germ theory of disease was nonsense. Physicians would just be revealed as quacks handing out placebos, gaining great wealth by manipulating our fears and false hopes. So it is today with the status of Christian leadership in many people's eyes.

In contrast, two modern ways of thinking currently carry great public allegiance and generate our most powerful systems of meaning, the worlds represented by the therapist and the manager.[5] Our society looks to management to control the external world and therapy the inner life. The confidence invested in these systems lifts them to the level of potential idols in our society. Both are capable of subverting the church.

THE THERAPEUTIC—CURING THE SOUL?

The therapeutic revolution owes something to the ideas of the Enlightenment in that the same sorts of scientific methodology developed in the hard sciences were applied to the study of human psychology as well. But it also owes a great deal to the social changes that sprang out of the Industrial Revolution. We are used to applying human techniques to hitherto unsolvable problems and coming up with solutions. Now we look to physicians—those with "professional" training—more than ministers for the cure of the soul.

Victims without Guilt

The human sciences hold great respect in our society, a good deal of it deserved. But much academic and popular psychology gives a different diagnosis and remedy for human problems than the historic Christian faith. For example, in much popular psychology the vocabulary of diagnosis includes words like codependency, dysfunction, addiction, denial, and low self-esteem. The vocabulary of growth includes self-fulfillment, self-realization, wholeness, integration, and high self-esteem.

These terms both contradict and overlap biblical ones in subtle and confusing ways. Let me give you a fairly extreme example of someone who understands himself within these therapeutic categories. This is a man who regularly beats up his girlfriend. While discussing the problem on a television talk show he was posed the question, "Why do you abuse her?"

> "I was on the receiving end of a lot of violence as a child—psychological and physical . . . my mother spanked me, my father hit me, the coach choked me—it's the way I was taught to handle my emotions. . . ."

"Will you marry? Or not see each other?"

"My first commitment is to my own growth. The main thing will be to build up my sense of self-esteem. If marriage fits into that, then I will get married, but if not, no. I'll just have to see."

We must say first that most psychologists would disapprove of this sort of attitude. But the man's outlook shows the impact the therapeutic revolution can have on the person in the street in ways that are likely to horrify psychologists of many different persuasions.

Notice how steeped this man is in the popular jargon of therapy. His final reality is self. Nothing beyond is important. Self-esteem is his immediate goal and the means to most other objectives. He has a concept of victimhood but no concept of guilt. Nonetheless, he is confident that he can work through his difficulties with the modern technologies of personal growth.

When Self-Esteem Reigns

The pressure on the Christian to compromise with the therapeutic mindset comes in two places. First, when we think in therapeutic categories we are less likely to offend others steeped in them. And second, we begin to view these techniques as offering the power to change ourselves and others. So what is the problem?

Truth becomes marginalized. What begins to matter is less what is true than what seems to help for healing, wholeness, and above all, self-esteem. If Christ is part of that, fine. But if Buddha helps, that's okay too. Or maybe we would feel much better about ourselves if we drove a Porsche and spent long weekends at exotic places. Christian truth is relegated to the background where it won't interfere with psychological well-being.

Sin treated as a serious problem is seen as therapeutically unhelpful. In historic Christianity, sin is something for which we are held responsible, even inexcusable, and for which we ourselves have no cure. This truth jars against optimistic therapeutic sensibilities that emphasize human goodness and competence in dealing with all of life's challenges.

Gary Trudeau mocks the Christian accommodation to the therapeutic:

Notice how in embracing the therapeutic, the Christian faith also becomes a consumer product: "Let's shop around some more."

If the main problem to be addressed is low self-esteem, then Christ need not have come to live on earth, much less die on the cross. Ideas like sin, repentance, and self-sacrifice sound pretty negative to therapeutic ears. They could spread self-doubt or even guilt and shame rather than promote self-esteem.

Our Deepest Need

Christian accommodation to the therapeutic may sound wonderful and warm, but it is a profound betrayal of the faith that we were meant to defend, not dilute. You can see the chameleon effect in a well-known Christian author's version of the first Beatitude: "Blessed are the self-esteemers, for they shall see the beauty of their own souls." This statement is possibly the direct opposite of what it means to be "poor in spirit," although it may be therapeutically correct.[6]

Another popular leader assures us that "The need for dignity, self-worth, self-respect, and self-esteem is the deepest of all human needs." Or as another leader says, "Reformational theology failed to make clear that the core of sin is a lack of self-esteem."[7]

Even many Christian organizations seem to assume that the highest good is feeling good about ourselves. Through their advertisements we are told to send money for third-world development ". . . and you will feel good about yourself," or to spend time with your children in order to "feel good about yourself." The reason to do what is good is no longer to please God or be obedient to him, but to improve one's self-esteem.

If we become chameleons, adapting to the coloring of the therapeutic revolution, then, to return to the original metaphor, we stand to lose our saltiness. I'm not denying the wisdom that we can learn from psychology and other human sciences. Simply rejecting them is sheer folly. But the challenge is to discern what is of value and what is not.

THE MANAGERIAL—THE BOTTOM LINE?

By the managerial we mean breaking down almost any aspect of the world, controlling specific variables, and working out the desired change. Clear and measurable goals are defined and specific procedures to realize them are implemented. While the therapeutic revolution aims at self-esteem, the managerial has as its goal efficiency and profit, a quantifiable bottom line.

This mode of meaning has changed the world in countless wonderful ways. The development of the industrial world has depended on it. Yet a good servant can be a brutal master when it becomes the dominant meaning system in life.

Measuring the Unmeasurable

What happens when the managerial mentality is brought into Christian experience, the Christian life, the Christian church? One might say that the Bible itself diagnoses problems and seeks solutions that are to be pursued with single-mindedness. Surely no one wants to accept inefficiency or financial irresponsibility.

The danger of accommodation, however, is that we can easily forfeit the depth and richness of knowing God for the shallowness of the commercial world—all without realizing it. At peril is our relationship to God and to other people.

Evangelicals have long thought of the life of faith in terms of clear and measurable goals. We can find step-by-step packages on how to witness, how to find the will of God, how to pray, how to receive the Holy Spirit, and on and on. Techniques suggest that success awaits us when we follow the easy-to-read instructions.

Expedience is the new master: "Adopt this plan of fundraising, church growth, or [even] worship—it gets results!" Certain practices are "shown to be effective," leading those who raise objections to seem negative and small-minded.

Or we incorporate the "positive thinking" needed to achieve corporate goals. For example, a friend of mine demonstrated the corporate world's self-confident rhetoric when mentioning that his ministry was moving to Dallas because it is a "can do" city. We can take this kind of bravado into our direct relationship with God where it is even more inappropriate.

But lost in the managerial mentality is concern for qualities of character, integrity, wisdom, and recognition of the nearly infinite varieties of unpredictability and brokenness in this world. These characteristics are not measurable nor can they be broken down and packaged. What is more, developing them would take too long in the managerial point of view.

The result is a trivializing of the nature of our relationship to God and the various ways he has given us to grow. We begin to believe that we have more control over our own growth than we actually do, which leads to less humility and less dependence on God. As with secularization in general, we acquire an inflated sense of our own power to produce change along with a corresponding sense of the irrelevance of God in his transcendence, grace, wisdom, and power. Perhaps unknowingly we subvert spirituality itself.

Compromise with the managerial meaning system may be most obvious in the way Christians understand Christian service. Evangelism is a clear example. One Christian leader writes, "There are five great laws of selling or persuading . . . . It does not matter whether you are selling a refrigerator or persuading men to accept a new philosophy, the same basic laws apply." Or another says, "We are selling a product, and that product is Jesus Christ."[8]

Managing specific elements in the process of evangelism involves every minute detail. For example, one guide to evangelism tells us, "Do smile, especially as you ask the two commitment questions. If you are too intense, your prospect may feel he is being pinned down, and resent it."[9]

For many, the main guide is the sort of market analysis that has shown itself to be so effective in advertising and selling commercial products. The measurable goal of evangelism is numbers of people, for it must be quantifiable to track success.

Yet an unintended consequence of this practice is that measuring success in ministry in terms of such visible categories transforms our own priorities. Wisdom, character, and the fruit of the Spirit are impossible to see, much less quantify, so they get pushed to the margins. People are treated less as whole persons than as pieces that must fit efficiently into the fulfillment of our criteria of success. Notice that a human person has become "your prospect."

Gaining Time, Losing Relationships

When Christian leaders adopt the managerial framework they become professionalized; the ideal leader is an effective manager or CEO. Leaders then become governed by considerations of efficiency in terms of time and money.

For example, I recently received an advertisement for a book containing "450 flawless model letters" for the busy pastor who is frustrated by the amount of time spent in letter writing. Notice the conception of the ministry implicit in these excerpts:

> Here, ready for use by you and your secretary, are no less than 450 excellent letters covering all kinds of situations that call for a message over your signature. They say just what you want to say in admirably clear and compelling language.
>
> 90% of their language is already in place; all you need to do is modify it slightly to finish the job. A letter that might normally take 30 or 40 minutes to draft can be completed, ready to mail in 5 minutes. . . .
>
> Here you have deeply moving appeals on behalf of needy parishioners, and families victimized by fire or other disaster. You have letters seeking support for a new building program, foreign missions, plant maintenance, church debt retirement, and other purposes. . . .
>
> Several letters, addressed to major benefactors who have given generously in the past, can produce very large gifts for you. Sooner or later, you'll surely have occasion to adapt them. . . .

Your time is at a premium; and since this book can save
you so much time, why not send for a copy right now?

What is the matter with this? In the meaning system of the
manager nothing is wrong; it cannot be faulted. Time is gained,
money is raised, and that ministry moves forward. In the larger
meaning system of the Bible, however, there is a great deal the
matter. It is pastoral care with the person removed. The leader
becomes so professionalized and hollowed out that what remains
is merely a veneer—the image—of a caring pastor.

Is this the model of leadership demonstrated by Jesus himself? No, it is Christian leadership without salt, as a chameleon
before the diluting forces of the commercial world.

Accommodation to the managerial meaning system can
involve the sacrifice of truth just as effectively as accommodation
to the therapeutic meaning system. If you want to make a sale,
why mention unpleasant or undesirable aspects of the product?
We are to be market driven, not product driven. But with the
Christian faith, we do not have to be very market driven to lose
the product entirely—and then what are we "selling"?

As we stand before the forces of managerial power, it is easy
to see that we can dilute our salt without knowing it. The
promises and powers of human technique can so dazzle us with
measurable results that appear to be real that we miss the unintended consequences.

BE TRANSFORMED, NOT CONFORMED

We have looked at some of the dangers of being a Christian
chameleon who adapts to our society's norms, values, and social
patterns. The forces on us are enormous, and all the more so
because of the everpresent danger of tribalism. How easy it is to
swing from saltless salt to light under a box, or even to be both at
the same time in different areas of our lives.

One of the tragic ironies is that, having allowed Christ to
be marginalized in modern society, we turn for help to some of
the very idols that marginalized him in the first place. In an

effort to reempower the church, pastors are often trained to be some combination of CEO and psychotherapist. A "successful" pastor is one who is a good generator of programs, a good fundraiser, and one skilled at public relations, demographic predictions, and modern communications. Success is determined by numbers and by making people feel good about themselves.

Could this success be through well-developed human capabilities but without the crucified and risen Christ? Jesus himself can be pushed to the margins by the very "success" of his followers.

Our call is not to be conformed to the world, but by grace to be transformed by God. This call is not to be static, but to move beyond rigidity and relativism, tribalism and compromise. It is not to resist all change, bury our heads, and dig in our feet. Rather it is a cry to be transformed by God in a changing world, yet without being conformed to its contemporary powers. What a challenge for the people of God!

3

∞

Tribal Life

WE HAVE LOOKED at the pressure to comply and accommodate to the wisdom of the world—saltless salt. We now turn to the other direction that Jesus warns us about—hidden light. This is the attraction of Christian tribalism, the seduction of the musk ox. In a world where we meet disapproval and scorn, if not persecution, we are tempted to retreat in defiance and spend time only with those who support, affirm, and agree with us.

While there is nothing wrong with racial and ethnic groups organizing themselves in tribal ways, God's people are to be salt and light; we are to be in the world but not of it. Jesus calls us to maintain our dissonant relationship to the world without rigidity or isolation from it.[1]

REASONS FOR SEPARATION

As with accommodation to the world, motivations good, bad, and mixed can drive us to tribalism. One is Christ's command that we exist in community. We are not meant to be lone rangers of the faith but are to have a real corporate life, not only because of our obligations to one another but also because of our need for support, encouragement, and accountability. Tribalism in the church is a perverting of the need for community.

The tendency toward tribalism usually begins with certain legitimate concerns and fears. For example, we are afraid that if we do not stand firmly on God's absolute truths, we will slide into compromise, then relativism, and finally to unbelief.

It is easy to see that this has happened theologically and ethically to the extent that it has not only weakened the church, but also the backbone of moral authority in our culture. Think of the many colleges and universities that began as Christian institutions to educate students for the purpose of better serving God. In many of them, the Christian faith is now ignored or the object of condescension. Religiously grounded points of view are subjected to the same intolerance that Christians leveled against secularism in an earlier age.[2]

Another legitimate fear is that of being overwhelmed by modern confusions rooted in our pluralistic society. We may try so hard to respect ambiguities that we end up never taking a stand on theological, moral, or political issues, even though our nation and world might be collapsing around us. This fear underlies a desire for clear and precise ways to understand the complicated issues of our time.

Polarization plays as major a role in being hidden light as it does for being saltless salt. It is easy to believe that we can only avoid the compromise of spineless accommodation by allying ourselves with those who stand with absolutism on absolutely everything. We start to see relativism as the one great danger that we must resist at all costs. Tribal Christian groups can be appealing by contrast to the loss of theological and moral authority in saltless churches.

Other motivations are less legitimate. Some people can give in to the fear that they might be argued out of their faith if they become involved personally with those who are not Christians. They instead keep a distance and remain only with those who agree. This seems a tacit surrender to unbelief.

Other people are attracted to the idea of a complete simplicity regarding right and wrong. Indignation and even hatred against "Secular Humanists," "New Agers," "Feminists," or the "Politically Correct" can feel satisfying. We can obtain a perverse pleasure out of a vision of life that enables us to localize total evil somewhere—elsewhere—on earth. Tribalism offers to satisfy these yearnings.

ISOLATION AND INSULATION

As we have seen, Christian tribalism usually occurs through a combination of motivations. It also results from intentional and unintentional practices, such as a church having so many weekly meetings that its members have little or no free time. Members are unable to relate to those outside of their fellowship group because they lead a church-occupied life. Some, of course, see such separation as a positive virtue, a measure of spiritual maturity.

What is Christian tribalism? Put simply, it is having little voluntary association with those who are not Christians, whether in recreation, social life, or friendship. Being surrounded by those who believe as we do affirms our own beliefs and self-confidence.

Christians in the tribal mode begin to speak in a tribal Christian dialect, using words and phrases that have not been in common conversation outside the church for over a hundred years. This dialect is a kind of conversational shorthand made up of Christian clichés, jokes, and tribal information, usually spoken without thought to the meaning. It can be uttered to businessmen and women found through the local Christian Yellow Pages, used to ensure that God's people do business only with those who are born-again.

Tribalism seems to discourage historical awareness and cultural diversity. Even Dickens and Shakespeare are sometimes excluded from the curriculum in Christian education.

In tribal life the future is ominous and the past contains a "Golden Age" that we seek to retrieve. Change is suspect, especially if it is culturally strange to us. These ideas do not bring a life-giving sense of tradition but a life-constricting one. It can seem to be betrayal of God himself if we dare to ask, "Could we have gotten it wrong?"

TRIBAL HAZARDS

At least two kinds of occupational hazards come with tribalism. One is an inflation in the number of rules. Although presented as moral issues, these new decrees are not really moral absolutes in the New Testament. The other is a toleration of evils that are offensive to God but comfortable to us because of their familiarity within our traditions. With this leniency can come the tendency to resist changes that God himself is working among his people.

Multiplying Rules

The ethics of the New Testament tolerate too much ambiguity to affirm a sense of tribal identity. They allow too much freedom for individuals to be led by God's Spirit in their own individuality and life context. But in a fast-changing world of moral disorientation, this freedom can be threatening.

Christians often want closure on as many moral ambiguities as possible: What music should a Christian listen to? What films should we watch? Whom should I marry? Precisely what is the decision-making process by which we know that we are in God's will?

Tribal Christians want to know the right way and wrong way on every issue and then teach it to others to keep them from going wrong. When in doubt it is safer to say "no" than "yes," for permission seems more dangerous than prohibition.

As rules are multiplied they will inevitably concern such external things as appearance, music, films, and checklists of political positions. But commands added to New Testament ethics are apt to fix on somewhat arbitrary practices and priorities. They might have had certain wisdom in earlier situations but they are anachronistic and destructive when turned into moral absolutes for all times and places.

One of the clearest examples of this tendency comes from an early nineteenth-century writer in England in a short work called

Cottage Economy. The author, William Cobbett, attacks the evils of drink:

> It must be evident to every one, that the practice . . . must render the frame feeble and unfit to encounter hard labour or severe weather. . . . Hence succeeds a softness, an effeminacy, a seeking for the fireside, a lurking in the bed, and . . . all the characteristics of idleness. . . . [Drinking] fills the public-house and makes the frequenting of it habitual, corrupts boys as soon as they are able to move from home, and does little less for the girls, to whom the gossip of the [drinking place] is no bad preparatory school for the brothel. At the very least, it teaches them idleness.[3]

We've probably heard similar accounts elsewhere. Interestingly, however, Cobbett is not writing against the evils of drinking alcohol, but against the evils of drinking tea. In fact, the little book is on making home-brewed beer, obviously a morally superior drink for the whole family.

Why was tea seen to be so dangerous? My hunch is that it was relatively new in that part of England. As this illustration shows, something quite arbitrary can acquire high moral importance if we are not suspicious of proliferating rules and if we have little perspective of history.

Cultural Blindness

The second hazard of tribalism occurs when our vision is too narrow. With a restricted outlook we are likely to be too comfortable with certain traditions that God does not tolerate. We overlook areas where the Bible demands reform because we read the Bible the way that those around us have always read it. Examples of this blindness are uncomfortably numerous in our own history. Some American Christians vigorously defended race-based slavery, and others opposed allowing women to vote—both on what they took to be biblical grounds.

Another example can be found in biblical studies. Matthew Henry was a wonderful eighteenth-century Puritan whose com-

mentary on the whole Bible is still one of the most valuable any-
where. But an illustration of his cultural blindness occurs in his
comments on the second chapter of the letter of James.

In this letter James discusses his concern that the Christian
not treat the rich with favoritism and the poor with neglect or
contempt. He uses an example to illustrate how not to treat rich
and poor as they arrive at a church meeting:

> My brothers and sisters, do you with your acts of favoritism
> really believe in our glorious Lord Jesus Christ? For if a person
> with gold rings and in fine clothes comes into your assembly,
> and if a poor person in dirty clothes also comes in, and if you
> take notice of the one wearing the fine clothes and say, "Have
> a seat here, please," while to the one who is poor you say,
> "Stand there," or, "Sit at my feet," have you not made dis-
> tinctions among yourselves, and become judges with evil
> thoughts (James 2:1–4)?

Henry explained this point very well. But he then went on
to qualify the application of the passage. He wrote:

> But we must be careful not to apply what is here said to the
> common assemblies for worship; for in these certainly there
> may be appointed different places for persons according to
> their rank and circumstances, without sin.[4]

Henry was assuring his readers that James's words about
social prejudice did not apply to the practice of their time still
under the influence of the feudal system. In those days the lord of
the manor had a pew in the front of the church with his name
on it for himself and his family. He would sit in this reserved
pew while his servants would have to find a seat in the gallery or
wherever they could. Prejudice on the basis of social rank had
become so culturally ingrained and institutionalized that it was
even built into the architecture of the churches.

When I first read Henry's comments I was taken aback, for
James's words apply so *exactly* to this practice. Even Henry was
too culturally captive to see James's message that Christ rela-
tivizes and challenges the hierarchies of class in a way that should

have shaken church life profoundly, not to mention the whole structure of society. But if such a great scholar and man of faith could make this mistake, how much more do we need to understand the Bible afresh in our time, listening to voices from outside of our immediate cultural experience.

The Dangers of Safety

One of the powerful appeals of Christian tribalism is its promise of safety. In a society where change happens at lightning speed and where nothing seems solid and fixed, the tribal arguments have real persuasiveness. But is the promise of safety really so sure? I would suggest that it simply offers a different set of dangers.

Why as a general rule would it be safer to say "no" than "yes" when we are in doubt? Why would it be safer to say "no" when God says "yes" than to say "yes" when God says "no"? I would suggest that nothing is safe about being more restrictive than God's word. In fact, it is pretty dangerous.

Often when rules multiply, those that occupy most of our attention are the least significant. "And why do you break the commandment of God for the sake of your tradition?" Jesus asked (Matthew 15:3). He spent much of his time showing how intricate Sabbath prohibitions blocked God's command to love one's neighbor.

I will always remember a L'Abri student who was the son of a pastor. He had been thrown out of his home by his father because "his hair was too long" and "he asked too many questions." Listening to his bitterness underlined for me the utter lack of safety in such priorities.

Protestant fundamentalism's many moral prohibitions— against playing cards, dancing, going to the cinema, or drinking even small amounts of alcohol—are difficult to find in the Bible. Yet in many circles they have been held with the full force of absolute moral principle. So many children growing up in such an environment find it so arbitrarily restrictive that they turn away. By adding moral absolutes to those in Scripture, we relativize the Bible and make it seem to be just part of a conser-vative ideological package.

The modern Roman Catholic Church faces the same strug-gles as its Protestant counterparts but with different issues. Large percentages of Catholics simply ignore the church's ban on birth control and many disagree with the prohibition of marriage for priests. The authority of the church to speak on moral issues is undercut in its members' eyes.

TO LOVE, CHERISH, AND STAY AT HOME?

Another example of the danger of thinking only of safety can be found in the identity and role of women in society, church, and family. In response to modern confusion, many conserva-tive Christians have defended what seems to be the safe "tradi-tional" view of men, women, and family. This is the belief that women should get married, be submissive to their husbands, stay with the children instead of working outside the home, be hum-ble, passive, never assertive, and exercise spiritual guardianship over the home. All of this comes as a moral package stamped with God's authority.

But if we look carefully, four quite different principles lie behind such a package. First, there are true biblical principles that bear on all human beings—husbands, wives, and all single people too—such as the need for humility, mutual submission, gentleness, and spiritual leadership. It is therefore misleading to see these principles as the special province of married women.

Second, there are biblical principles that apply to all wives (to be submissive to their husbands), but need to be seen in the setting of mutual submission of all Christians to each other (including husbands to their wives).[5]

Third, the prohibition against women working outside of the home has no Scriptural authority but is merely one response to industrialization. In the mid-nineteenth century there was a new division of labor for middle- and upper-class women. Men went out to work and women stayed at home. But in the millennia before the Industrial Revolution almost nobody worked outside of the home. After it, poor women had no chance to stay at home even if they wanted to.

And fourth, some parts of the package are simply sinful and defy biblical teaching. They are chauvinistic expectations for women such as the belief that women should be passive and never be assertive.

What is dangerous about this package as a whole is that it goes under the banner of a biblical position to be held faithfully against feminist attacks on the family. It leads people to associate time-bound, culture-bound, and even sinful principles and practices with the teaching of the Bible.

Not surprisingly, for many it has been the occasion to reject the whole of the Christian faith from a platform of perceived moral superiority. The ranks of radical, lesbian feminism are littered with bitter fundamentalist Christian dropouts.

For others this outlook has been used to justify sin as if it were the only faithful biblical response. We can think of husbands who even see it as their responsibility to keep their wives "in line" by physical abuse with "biblical" justification.

There is no safety on any of these issues apart from carefully separating out God's absolutes from those things that might be wise in one cultural setting but not in another. And we must distinguish those strands from practices that are actually sinful in any setting. To separate these themes we need all the biblical understanding that we can get, coupled with knowledge of our own historical context.

IS THERE A CHRISTIAN JIHAD?

Tribal hatred is not characteristic of all tribal Christians, but it is becoming more of a temptation for all marginalized groups, Christians included. One social critic described the appeal of the jihad:

> Jihad delivers . . . a vibrant local identity, a sense of community, solidarity among kinsmen, neighbors, countrymen, nar-

rowly conceived. But it also guarantees parochialism and is
grounded in exclusion. Solidarity is secured through war
against outsiders.[6]

Certain tribal scenarios say that things are so far gone and
society is so far decayed that we should suspend Jesus' teaching
on love, particularly on love for one's enemy. To require love at
all times is seen as impractical, given the extremity of the battle.
If we have located pure and complete evil, we no longer need
to treat those who disagree with us with love and humility. Anyone who is unashamed of Christ will join the culture wars with
all their energy—and hatred.

It must be said that the rhetoric of holy war can be good for
fund-raising within the tribal fortress. But it is not good for those
who believe that Jesus' command to love our enemies still stands,
or for those who struggle to put into practice the Christian calling to try to persuade those who disagree—whether the issues
be spiritual or political.

Christians have developed a reputation for scorning and
ridiculing anyone on the other side of the battle lines of the culture wars, whether they be politicians, academics, or neighbors.
This has created an environment of needless hostility where
there is already tension aplenty. Too often Christians have
walked with all four feet into the secular culture's stereotype of us
as bigoted and unwilling to listen.

The tribal mistake is not that Christians have taken moral
principles into the political arena and fought hard for them.
This is our responsibility. Rather the error is that within a tribal
attitude of jihad, God's commandments to love are scorned or
forgotten.

If in our main forays outside the tribal fortress we are trying
to overpower our neighbors politically by fair means and foul,
and if we have exempted ourselves from Jesus' command to love
our neighbor and our enemy, what becomes of the mission of
the church? How great is our desire to spread the gospel? How
believable is our message?

Of course Christians sometimes live in settings of enormous political and spiritual evil—it is hard not to think of Christians in our century living under Nazism or Communism. In these situations resistance is called for, but conditions vary so much that it is impossible to prescribe responses ahead of time or in some generalized way.

FREEDOM WITHIN THE ABSOLUTES

The apostle Paul's example of dealing with different forms of tribalism in the Corinthian church is instructive for us today. One problem Paul was facing was the Corinthians' warped picture of the kind of separation from the world that God wanted. He wrote to correct their misunderstanding:

> I wrote to you in my letter not to associate with sexually immoral persons—not at all meaning the immoral of this world, or the greedy and robbers, or idolaters, since you would then need to go out of the world. But now I am writing to you not to associate with anyone who bears the name of brother or sister who is sexually immoral or greedy. . . (1 Corinthians 5:9–11).

The idea of personal separation from the pagan world and its sins was shocking to Paul. To do so one would have to leave the planet—or isolate oneself in a tribal group. What he meant instead was that those who claimed to be Christians should be held to the whole standard of Christ and should be disciplined if they stubbornly held to these sins. Paul's lifelong passion was to bring the gospel of God's grace to the idolater, immoral, and greedy—to those outside.

We see another side of tribalism in Paul's discussion of the observance of different days, whether to eat specific foods as well as whether to eat meat that had been sacrificed to idols. He deals with these issues in 1 Corinthians 10:14–32 and Romans 14.

The matter of eating food previously sacrificed to idols turned out to be quite complex. It was certainly wrong to worship an idol because it was a false god and to worship it was to betray the true God. But it was just as certainly permitted that we can eat all foods, for ". . . the earth and its fullness are the Lord's" (1 Corinthians 10:26). Eating meat that someone else might have sacrificed to an idol is not the same as worshipping the idol yourself.

For some Christians, however, eating meat that had been sacrificed was seen as a betrayal of God, and was probably related to longstanding tensions between Jew and Gentile. For some, eating sacrificed meat seemed to be the thin end of the wedge that got them back into idolatry.

The safest, clearest, most unambiguous thing for Paul to do would have been to say, "You can't eat meat sacrificed to idols under any circumstances." This line of thinking would include the idea that people shouldn't be confused with moral subtleties; they should just hear a clear "no" and that would reduce the risk of them falling back into idolatry. But this was not Paul's approach.

The apostle wanted to guard other priorities as well as the safety of the Christian's clear-cut moral agenda. The food itself was part of God's world and there was nothing wrong with eating it. He was also concerned that if people were eating with those who were not believers and were offered meat, that they would not make a moral issue out of a peripheral point and cause unnecessary offense.

Paul resisted the temptation to give one fixed answer for all people in all occasions. He said that it was permissible to eat the meat, except when it might lead another person astray. Then one should not eat it—out of love for the person, not because of the wrongness of the act itself. The law of love was brought in as an absolute, overriding our freedom.

This is a wonderful example of New Testament faith in action. Life is complicated. The world is bent out of shape. Things are not simple. But we do have certain absolutes to live by and within them we have great freedom.

In the context of discussing Christian freedom to value different days differently, Paul wrote, "Let all be fully convinced in their own minds" (Romans 14:5). Imagine that—he did not expect all Christians to agree. Most of the rest of that chapter is spent telling Christians to let others make up their own minds and follow their own consciences on the issues not involving biblical absolutes.

The force of this discussion makes clear that God himself must be our source of security. We must not seek our sense of well-being in freedom from disapproval or persecution—either by being a chameleon or a tribal musk ox. There is plenty of room for close fellowship, support, and tradition, without the need to tribalize.

Part 2

Pressure Points
for Transformation

4

⚮

The Recovery of Apologetics

WE HAVE LOOKED at some of the destructive effects of the Christian failure to be salt and light. The chameleon–musk ox polarization cripples the Christian life, leading on the one hand to a take-it-or-leave-it attitude to the word of God and on the other to a desire to multiply moral commandments beyond the Bible.

This polarization makes fulfilling Jesus' Great Commission— to make disciples of all nations—almost impossible to carry out. The chameleon thinks, "Well, what's the use of spreading the gospel? It isn't all that different from what people believe already and it's so divisive. Why not leave those who aren't Christians in peace?" The musk ox, in contrast, may feel the urgency of evangelism but neither knows anyone outside the walls of the tribal fortress nor speaks the local language.

How can we respond to the dilemma raised by the opposing forces? What can we do to prevent being drawn into the polarization? How can we stop the bleeding that it has already caused the body of Christ?

When our human bodies are losing blood from an artery, we do not try to stop the bleeding by pressing on the surface of our whole body, but only on certain pressure points. Similarly, to stop the hemorrhaging of the body of Christ, we need to apply pressure at certain points where attention and hard work will bring wide and deep results over time. Although we could explore any number of specific pressure points, I will restrict the discussion to two.

The recovery of apologetics is one such pressure point. Another is the development of the church as a nontribal community. These issues, and the biblical foundation beneath them, will be our focus in part 2.

THE PROCESS OF PERSUASION

"Apologetics" may be an unfamiliar word—what does it mean? Put simply, apologetics is the defense of the Christian faith. The term was used by the apostles to describe a response made to an unbeliever who inquires about, criticizes, or attacks the Christian faith.[1] The word also carries the force of giving both an answer and a positive challenge to one who does not believe in Christ.

Apologetics is a critical and indispensable part of evangelism. Sometimes it is not necessary, as when the Philippian jailer asked the apostle Paul, "What must I do to be saved?" Paul's response was simply, "Believe in the Lord Jesus, and you will be saved. . ." (Acts 16:30–31). In this instance Paul did not need to persuade or employ arguments; this time, however, was an exception. Usually he had to argue, discuss, dialogue, and persuade his hearers—whether they were Jews or Gentiles.

Paul never assumed that the people he encountered would understand and accept a simple proclamation of the claims of Christ. Since the Jews believed the Hebrew Scriptures, Paul persuaded them to believe in Jesus by using the Old Testament references to the coming Messiah.[2] To persuade the Gentiles, who did not believe in the Hebrew Scriptures but who worshiped a variety of idols, he interacted with their own ideas about nature and human moral and religious experience.[3]

The apostle Paul had obviously listened carefully to the ideas, fears, and dreams of people with whom he spoke. His strategy of persuasion had a negative aspect, as he sought to disenchant them with the ideas that they might have believed all their lives; but it also had a positive aspect as he showed them that the claims of Christ were true and demanded a response of faith. Paul saw the need and prayed for the work of the Holy Spirit to open people's eyes, but throughout his life he still took the trouble to learn about those with whom he was speaking.

Paul's ministry was known not just for preaching and letter-writing, but for two-way interaction, just as the ministry of Jesus before him. For example, in Corinth he "argued in the synagogue every Sabbath, and persuaded Jews and Greeks" (Acts 18:4, RSV). He went on to Ephesus where he "entered the synagogue and for three months spoke boldly, arguing and pleading about the kingdom of God" (Acts 19:8, RSV). When the Jews in the synagogue finally threw him out, he left and rented a hall in which he "argued daily. . . . This continued for two years, so that all the residents of Asia heard the word of the Lord, both Jews and Greeks" (Acts 19:10, RSV).

Paul did not merely preach a sermon and then go home. Instead he listened to his hearers and interacted with their ideas, beliefs, objections, questions, gripes, doubts, and struggles. He took his hearers seriously, respecting and loving them.

The apostle's experience as recorded in the book of Acts is similar to our own today. We too meet people who believe, often with deep conviction, in completely different ideas about God, truth, and humanity. They may also have very sophisticated reasons for not believing in Christ or the Bible. What should we do? Just keep proclaiming the truth of Christ in a louder voice? I don't think so.

Both apostles, Paul and Peter, taught that apologetics should be done with respect and gentleness, not with a spirit of contention or confrontation. Part of the spiritual battle is lovingly to ". . . destroy arguments and every proud obstacle raised up against the knowledge of God. . ." (2 Corinthians 10:5) and give a "defense to anyone who demands from you an accounting for the hope that is in you" (1 Peter 3:15).

Christians need not be the best debaters nor have all the answers—in fact, if we appear to know everything we will surely be viewed with suspicion. But we must have some of the answers that we can express in terms comprehensible to non-Christians, and plenty of good questions. We need to make every effort to learn about what people believe, why they believe it, how we can challenge those beliefs and present the gospel of Christ with humility. This is nothing less than a life-long challenge.

WHAT HAPPENS WITH NO APOLOGETICS?

What happens when apologetics are not practiced? In short, the polarization between compromise and tribalism, relativism and rigidity, will almost certainly triumph. The failure of apologetics can either lead to or flow from either pole—chameleon or musk ox.

A sharp apologetic will include an understanding of the surrounding culture, such as its hopes, habits, fears, idols, social structures, and basic ideas. It will also include a grasp of the way these ideas and practices interact with biblical truth. At what points do biblical faith and today's ideas and ways collide? Where is there friction? And where is there some commonality, and therefore possible points for conversation or cooperation?

If we have not thought these issues through clearly, we may find ourselves on the wrong side of battles without realizing it. For example, many of the mainline Protestant churches have tended to be too uncritical of secular high culture, such as ideas and values propagated in higher education and the arts. They have become saltless, chameleons who have adapted their views of truth, God, and humanity to the accepted wisdom of the time.

In contrast, the more evangelical and fundamentalist churches have tended to be too uncritical of popular culture, such as the views of truth and the value of the marketplace, entertainment, and the psychological self-help movement.[4] Both sides have been chameleons in their own ways through lack of critical engagement with the world's ideas and practices.

But without a vital apologetic, another problem will arise, namely fear. Those in the evangelical and fundamentalist direction are especially vulnerable to the seductiveness of tribalism here. Some feel no confidence about responding to non-Christian gripes, difficulties, questions, and arguments. They may have never considered these grievances and may fear that facing them would weaken their own faith. Thus contact with non-Christians becomes either diffident and timid or belligerent and bombastic.

The recovery of biblical apologetics works against the ignorance and the confusion that makes chameleon accommodation so easy to slip into. And it also works against the fear that makes the safety of musk-ox tribalism seem so appealing. Carried out with love and respect, apologetics is one way of overcoming the polarization that divides.

MODERN BLOCKS TO CHRISTIAN CREDIBILITY

At this point it would be valuable to describe the whole task of apologetics, which, alas, is far beyond the scope of this book. Instead we will focus on just a few of the major blocks to believing in the Christian faith today.

As we speak to people and try to understand where they are before the truth of God, certain issues emerge again and again. Some are up-front and in our face; others are more beneath the surface and less often articulated but just as powerful. In this chapter we will look at five areas that are intertwined with each other: modern relativism, postmodern suspicion, the implausibility of transcendence, the loss of belief in sin, and the conviction that the Christian faith is the enemy of life.

We will then explore the first issue—modern relativism—in more depth in the next chapter, giving ways to address it apologetically. But because space precludes adequate answers to the other issues here, I will include a valuable apologetics bibliography for them in the appendix.

Modern Relativism

The idea that the Bible is a unique revelation of God or that Jesus is the only way to him is anathema to many people today. It is unthinkable to them because it seems intolerant, which by their standards makes it self-evidently false.

Relativism carries great persuasiveness in our society of increasingly diverse religious groups. Its roots, however, go back to the Enlightenment, and it is an important doctrine of modernism. This worldview held that human beings through their reason and experience were self-sufficient and could know and do what was good without the need for God. Religion was superstition that sometimes served a useful purpose of propagating morality and social cohesion; more often, however, it was seen as divisive and fanatical. The main human task was to create a more just, prosperous, and well-educated society. For this purpose, our religion should be kept to ourselves. When Christians try to persuade others to believe in Christ, they violate late twentieth-century relativistic protocol.

Postmodern Suspicion

Postmodernism does not just take a stand against the claims of the New Testament but against any profession to know absolute or objective truth. The postmodernist looks at the time-honored conflict between the theist and the atheist and says that both are naive to think they know either God's existence or absence.

The postmodern claim is that beneath all ultimate beliefs and ideals (including the secular ideals such as Progress, Liberalism, and Justice) is the quest to gain or retain power—especially in terms of race, class, sex, or ethnicity. Religious and philosophical ideas and ideals are used to cover up and legitimize the true self-interest and desire for power that is at the root of all of our motivations.

Since postmodernism holds in suspicion all ultimate truths and ideals, no truth can be known for sure. We can know only what seems to work at the present moment. We do not even know our own minds. The result is a suspicion or cynicism about all knowing. In this setting, reliable knowledge of God becomes out of reach to the point of being unthinkable.

It is not just God who is suspect. All ultimate meanings are seen as deodorants to cover the smell of our own self-interest. Ideals disguise our self-interest from others, but perhaps more importantly, from ourselves. They enable us to enjoy self-respect as we pursue selfishness.

But the postmodern style is not to despair. Instead there is often a lightheartedness because it feels good to give up trying to do something that is impossible to do anyway. The flavor of this attitude is clear in a piece by Frank Gannon in the *New York Times*:

> Something in the human mind says it's hopeless: The existence of God is something that human beings can never entirely discount, or entirely prove. Why torture yourself trying to answer a question like that? Get a hobby. Work out regularly. Eat low fat. Forget about what Yeats called "vague immensities."
>
> . . .Yet something deep in your soul says, Go ahead. Seek the ultimate answers. Maybe the human brain *can* actually know transcendent divinity. Yeah. Good one. Don't hurt yourself, O.K.?[5]

The challenge of postmodernism to the Christian faith is obvious. Postmodernists see Christian belief working as a smoke-screen for selfish motivations that Christians would be ashamed of, if they were aware of them. If the Christian faith really functions this way, its truth claims cannot be taken very seriously, let alone believed for their persuasiveness. Better to make a joke of the whole tragic attempt to know God.

The Implausibility of Transcendence

Our society has trouble taking transcendence seriously. Two very different factors contribute to this modern problem. One is that our society envelopes us in impermanence. In an everchanging world it is difficult to trust in the importance of anything beyond the immediate excitements and dangers. The other is that many

high-visibility expressions of the Christian faith do little to suggest a transcendent dimension.

Impermanence is all around us: Families are no longer a
bedrock source of stability and security. More and more children
live apart from their two biological parents, and those who are
significant in their lives are not constant. Mobility is extraordinary, so fewer and fewer people are tied to any one place. Local
communities have been broken up with the rush to jobs in cities,
and then from city to city. What in all of this is trustworthy?

We are also continually hammered by the powerful demands
of the consumer culture: Entertainment bathes us twenty-four
hours a day, from museums to mudwrestling. Images and information bombard us from all over the world through radio, television, telecommunications, and print. All of this is immediate,
subject to change, demanding all of our attention, and giving
no hint of anything lying beyond the material world. So much
seems important and pressing that there is little room for the
transcendent dimension. Within this setting of impermanence,
the Christian faith can appear too trivial to be true.

The Christian claim, of course, is anything but trivial, for
we believe that individuals and the whole community have actually met the transcendent God—the Creator of heaven and
earth—who in turn is deeply concerned for us and even loves
us. This infinite and personal Creator God has made himself
known to us through his own Son joining the human race. He
has opened the way for us—tiny, fragile, bent, twisted people—
to know him. And he is committed to our well-being even to
the point of forgiving us for sin and granting us life forever.
Whether one thinks these claims are true or not, it is impossible
to consider them trivial.

But do Christians look like people who have been in contact
with such a God? Are these claims believable to a generation
steeped in postmodern suspicion? What evidence do we show
of our personal relationship with an unimaginably great Being
outside of this world order? If we seem to be just like everyone
else in our thoughts, speech, possessions, priorities, and behavior,

we make mockery of our Christian claims. Those who say that God is a human invention will seem to have the far more plausible explanation.

Related is the second factor, the lack of transcendence evident in the lives of Christian leaders. When the highest visibility Christian leaders are getting into sexual and financial scandals and their message is the oft-repeated chorus, "Send me money for God's work," what are people to conclude? Or if the Christian message heard across the nation is essentially, "Believe in Jesus and you will feel good about yourself," what are serious inquirers to think?

If Christians seem to be "into Jesus" not as one who is ultimately True, but as an engaging hobby like an exercise regimen, what are non-Christians to make of our claims to contact with a transcendent God? In other words, if the church has become saltless and behaves as chameleon, it will show the world nothing that justifies belief in its extraordinary claims. People looking for signs of transcendence will see only human artifice and shallowness—in short, smoke, mirrors, and pleading.

If, on the other hand, the church shows to the world a tribal musk-ox ghetto, no challenge will be given either. The people of God will be explainable as a marginalized subculture who carve out their territory for their own self-protection. They will be seen as those who are involved in society only as much as they need to press for the advancement of their own group interests. The great Christian claims will be seen only as the extreme and grandiose rhetoric necessary to keep the tribe together.

Loss of the Belief in Sin

Belief in the idea of sin, as taught in the Bible, is deeply implausible today—in part a necessary result of the three points we have just made. If no transcendent God as Judge exists who has revealed good and evil to us, then who can say what sin is or who it is against? If our ideas about God and ultimate moral truth are merely human constructions, then why should they have any authority over us? In this setting, the idea of sin is seen to encourage joylessness, uptightness, inhibition, manipulation, self-righteousness, cruelty, disdain for culture, and lack of self-esteem. Who wants all that?

The implausibility of sin is also strengthened by modern views of human nature. Strong voices from within the human sciences claim that sin is an archaic notion. The reality of human choice itself is under heavy fire from psychology, sociology, neuroscience, evolutionary psychology, and computer science. And claims from within these fields hold that human attitudes and actions are at least potentially explainable by biological factors that we are not aware of, let alone able to control. The idea of being held morally accountable to God is therefore seen as barbaric and dependent on obsolete and negative moral categories.

But sin is not a peripheral Christian teaching. It is the biblical diagnosis of the most basic human problem, to which Jesus is the solution in his atoning death on the cross—and the only reason why he had to go to the cross at all.

Charges against Christianity

Finally, let us look at the common conception that the Christian faith is against what is best and most precious in life itself. I will simply list ten typical charges, each which overlap to some degree with the four previous points but need to be taken seriously in their own right. Any one of them could keep someone from bothering to investigate the reality of Christ.

1. The Christian faith is the enemy of pleasure, enjoyment, and fulfillment. It stands for inhibition, prohibition, insecurity, and self-righteousness.

2. The Christian faith is the enemy of democracy and civility. Conservative Christians want political power to create a theocracy with places in leadership only for those who agree with them.

3. The Christian faith is the enemy of women. From the early history of the church, leaders established the infe-

rior status of women in church and society and have resisted attempts to reform ever since.

4. The Christian faith is the enemy of gay people, as can be seen in the bumper sticker of a few years ago, "Kill a gay for Jesus."

5. The Christian faith is the enemy of cultural diversity; it is an ethnocentric moral police force.

6. The Christian faith is the enemy of non-white races. This has been evident from a theological defense of race-based slavery to the starting of Christian schools as a way to avoid the integration of the public school system.

7. The Christian faith is the enemy of the environment. The biblical notion of dominion over the earth is at the root of our abuse of the natural world.

8. The Christian faith is the enemy of the arts. Christians have scorned the world of the arts as either Satanic or trivial and have produced nothing of artistic value for a hundred fifty years.

9. The Christian faith is the enemy of science, education, and the advance of knowledge.

10. The Christian faith is the enemy of economic justice. It is a good religion for the fat cats who can interpret the Bible to legitimize their wealth and privilege.

I have heard all of these charges and many more from people who see themselves as morally superior to Christians. The charges themselves represent a vast mixture of understandable grievances, misunderstandings, and complete falsehoods. If left to stand, they provide enormous deterrents for people to give the Christian faith serious consideration. But they are standard public discourse today, especially in media and higher education.

If you are a Christian, perhaps you can feel the polarizing forces working on you as you read the ten charges. The chameleon voice speaks and says, "Well, I guess there is a lot of truth there. Maybe we must just apologize for past wrongs and avoid offending the consensus in the future." The timid musk-ox voice then tells you, "Keep a low profile. Don't risk getting caught in any divisive discussions like that." But the more defiant musk-ox voice might say, "Those claims are ridiculous. I can prove to anybody how stupid they are!" All these responses deny our identity as salt and light.

A Christian apologetic at the end of the twentieth century must not hide from issues. It must engage them not just to answer the attacks, but also to give challenges back in God's name and in his love. If no such response is made, that failure will lead to both accommodation and tribalism.

MAKING TRUTH KNOWN

Most of these challenges and grievances assert that the Christian faith is morally inferior to its alternatives. Many of them are also based on misunderstandings of biblical theology and morality. To answer responsibly one must be faithful to biblical teaching and Christian history while also returning a persuasive challenge for faith in Christ. This is no small task.

As these grievances suggest, the Christian faith has been blamed for almost every abomination and injustice that Western culture has produced. Is this true, untrue, or partially true? When are we dealing with Jesus himself and when are we coming up against what misguided or malicious people have done in the name of Christ?

Unless we do a certain amount of homework on the critical issues of contemporary concern we will not know how or where to enter the discussion. We need to know our own theology and history well or we will not know what to defend and what to repudiate.

Once we have thought through a biblical view of God, truth, and humanity we then have another task. We must figure out how to present those truths in the most persuasive way to someone who does not already believe them. One temptation is to bend the truth to fit the sensitivities of our hearers and fall into the chameleon pattern. The other temptation is to avoid the issue of plausibility and instead be satisfied if we have stated what is formally true. This of course is the musk-ox syndrome that avoids involvement in the lives, hopes, fears, and gripes of those who do not believe in Christ.

Some of the best apologists in the history of the church did not see themselves as apologists first but primarily as theologians and pastors. But they always thought apologetically. That is, they thought, spoke, and wrote with a concern for how biblical truth sounds in the ear of those who are not believers. Think, for example, of the writing of Augustine, Luther, Calvin, and Spurgeon. Like them, we must labor to take the truth that we have found and state it in fresh and compelling ways.

Historian John Kilner states the problem well:

> There is a tremendous reluctance to go the second intellectual mile. Many people exhaust themselves developing explicitly biblical positions on issues. They stop short of taking the next step of developing arguments for those positions in language that society is willing to consider. Others, anticipating the difficult challenge of developing socially persuasive arguments, simply skip the first step of formulating an explicitly biblical account. The first group is not likely to engage the society with their thoroughly biblical concerns. The second group is not likely to have thoroughly biblical concerns with which to engage society."[6]

Kilner is dealing with the very same polarization that we have described, as well as calling for an informed, apologetically sensitive speaking and writing. If we have no firm grasp on the truth, then our ideas are not God's, however effectively we may get them into the marketplace. And if there is no concern to persuade, whatever truth of God that we might have remains as light under a box.

The prospect of what we need to know might be enough to make some of us give up. Who has the time? But what matters most is that Christians would become people who are straining to grow in this direction.

REFRAMING APOLOGETICS

The apologetics that I am pleading for must not be seen as a narrow, argumentative activity occupying itself with fine-tuned technical discussion. Rather what I am calling for could be termed "cultural apologetics" because of its concern to engage people in the full breadth of their cultural understanding and participation.

Today's society can seldom hear or engage in our direct frontal arguments about God's existence or the historical evidence for the resurrection of Jesus. We have yet to get their attention. As Jesus and Paul did before us, we must be creative and imaginative in presenting God's truth.

One of the most effective apologists to the English-speaking world in our century has been C. S. Lewis (1898–1963). He wrote direct apologetic argument in the early 1940s but then shifted to write narrative with an apologetic edge to it.

Another was G. K. Chesterton (1874–1936), one of the most versatile of all recent apologists. Along with direct argument he also wrote history, biography, poetry, drama, novels, and short stories, all the while earning his living as a journalist. In his own exuberant style throughout he commends the humanness, sanity, humor, and fullness of the Christian life.

Would that we would raise up more apologists like Lewis and Chesterton. But the task for all Christians is to be who they are, yet to be people in motion. We who do not know all the answers should model the One who did: He gave few answers but asked many good questions and told unsettling stories. Through these, Jesus called long-held assumptions into doubt and planted seeds of faith in the minds and hearts of people who had been quite closed to his message.

It is not necessary nor even remotely desirable that all Christians get graduate degrees in philosophy, apologetics, or training in debating. What is necessary and desirable is that Christian people both know their own faith and take the ideas of their non-Christian friends seriously. Christians should be caring, curious people whose love for their friends and neighbors drives them to listen to and learn about what those friends and neighbors live for.

With this in mind, we turn to one of the most difficult issues of apologetics in our time. It is a discussion in which our own attitudes of humility and compassion will have as much to do with our ultimate effectiveness as our well-framed arguments.

5

∞

One Truth, One Way

OF ALL THE APOLOGETIC ISSUES RAISED, probably the one most common and difficult is the confrontation of modern relativism with the claim of Christ's uniqueness—that he is the only way to the one God. In looking at the challenge posed by this controversial discussion we will separate it into two questions.

First is the charge, "How can the Christian be so arrogant as to claim to know ultimate truth, meaning that others' truth claims are false when different from the Christian's?" And second, "Why do Christians insist on the uniqueness of Christ for salvation?" These questions could be summarized simply as, "Why only one truth?" and "Why only one way?"

WHY ONLY ONE TRUTH?

In delving into the matter of "why only one truth" we will examine three words—pluralism, relativism, and tolerance—that have been the source of spectacular confusion. As we begin, some functional definitions are helpful: Pluralism is simply a social fact; relativism is a philosophical doctrine that offers one of several possible interpretations of pluralism; and tolerance is a personal attitude and a social policy regarding the way we treat people who hold different beliefs from our own.

71

In putting forth these definitions I am fully aware that not everybody agrees with them. But if they did our discussions would have more clarity.

Pluralism and Relativism

Religious pluralism in Western Culture is a social reality—today we are surrounded by a plurality of religious beliefs and institutions. We may or may not like it, but this fact is difficult to deny. We live beside many Christian and Jewish groups, along with the full range of world religions and secular worldviews.

Relativism is not a social reality but a far-reaching philosophical doctrine. It offers one among several possible interpretations of pluralism. How do we understand the different truth claims, many of which seem mutually exclusive? Are all of them true? None true? Some more true than others? True only when they're all mixed together? Answers to these questions are not self-evident.

Relativism makes both negative and positive claims. On the negative side it says that no single religion or philosophy can know absolute truth because that is beyond human grasp. This is not just the statement that exhaustive knowledge of ultimate things is impossible for human beings—a claim that would startle no one. Rather it is the idea that true statements about the existence and character of God, and of moral right and wrong, are simply beyond the scope of human understanding and language.

The relativist claims that we cannot know if our statements correspond to reality; for example, we cannot know if what we say about God relates to who God actually is, if any God exists. No transcultural standard exists by which religions can be judged for their truthfulness.

One of the best-known proponents of this view is the theologian John Hick. He writes that all religions grasp for the Real, but that the Real is beyond all human concepts: "Thus it cannot be said to be one or many, person or thing, conscious or unconscious, purposive or non-purposive, substance or process, good or evil, loving or hating."[1] Hick, at least at this point, faces up to the full relativistic position—that God, if he exists, cannot be said to prefer even good to evil, love to hate.

Positively, relativism says that the claims that people do make about absolute truth are in fact only true "relative to" the local cultural and the psychological factors that produced them. These truth claims are attempts by individuals and groups to name what is unnamable from within their own limited perspective. The content of the beliefs is not important, because it is just the byproduct of the culture and situation in which they arose.

If we accept these doctrines we no longer speak of certain religious ideas being true and others false. All are more or less helpful at doing the same job, expressing human longings for the absolute and providing social and psychological stability. We do not talk of chocolate ice cream being true ice cream and vanilla being false just because we have always preferred chocolate to vanilla.[2] Both fulfill the same function in slightly different ways. So also is it ridiculous to use truth and falsehood as measures of religion. The only "wrong" that we are likely to commit is to be judgmental of the beliefs of others.

No Relativizing of Relativism

As we have seen, the cutting edge of the relativist's critique of religion is to say that all ultimate religious beliefs are properly understood not as possible sources of accurate knowledge about God and ourselves, but only as products of a culture's groping to name what cannot be named. At the same time, however, relativism claims for itself unique immunity from its own critique.

We are meant to have faith that relativism alone escapes the effect of relativizing factors in its own (modern, Western, academic, tenure-seeking) culture. It is meant to be mysteriously, objectively, timelessly true, coming to us as if through an epistemological immaculate perception.

This is the "overbite" of relativism. This doctrine can sound very humble one minute, as if only the relativist has honestly taken human fallibility into account. But then the next minute relativism speaks as if it has received a vision of ultimate truth and we should therefore accept its claim to be the view by which every other view is understood.

Relativism Destroys Pluralism

Although we may think of relativism embracing and celebrating pluralism, it actually does no such thing. Let me give you an example. You have probably heard of the illustration of religious relativism, that the various world religions are each a different road going up the same mountain. Although the travelers along the roads cannot see others who are climbing up the mountain, to their surprise they all meet at the top, that is, at God. This picture seems to illustrate a fair-minded, nonjudgmental, and enlightened approach to the plurality of religions, but in reality it is deceptive.

The one who accepts this illustration has actually created an over-religion, a paradigm that claims to interpret all religions and how they relate to each other. As the one lens through which all others are seen, this worldview is anything but relativistic. Instead it is an absolute claim to know about all absolute claims to truth.

We must ask where the observer stands who tells us of this picture. Such a one cannot be a mere human traveler trudging up the mountain with vision limited by his or her perspective; rather, to describe this whole scene, one has to be in an airplane to be able to see it. He or she claims a God's-eye view while remaining a finite, fallible human being. How is it that only the relativist has access to an airplane?

And what happens to the plurality of religions? It disappears as worldviews are no longer understood in terms of their distinctive ideas and practices, but are seen only to be the blind gropings of different cultures toward some Absolute. Relativism allows plurality only at the level of private or community opinion, which has no public factual status. Yet it insists on uniformity regarding its own view of ultimate truth, which does have public factual status. Thus relativism is really closet absolutism, although it scorns absolutism as naive, arrogant, and ethnocentric.

Relativism is also more high-handed than high-minded. To say that the Christian faith (which professes belief in a personal God) and Buddhism (which denies a personal God and is equivocal about belief in an impersonal God) are really the same in their most basic convictions denies the plurality that exists. It is an imposition of uniformity from on high. What emerges is not only that the Christian believes in absolutes, but that the relativist does too. The Christian, however, admits it.

The Christian faith holds that nonexhaustive but real knowledge of the ultimate truths of God is possible, but not because Christian people are the best thinkers. The Christian recognizes that there is one truth because God has in fact revealed himself in human language. God alone, who is at the top of the mountain, has a God's-eye view, and he has communicated to us in words.

The Seductiveness of Relativism

Why are such words as "conversion," "proselytize," "missionary," or "born again" now so offensive? Why should the most all-encompassing area of truth be off limits to honest discussion?

If pluralism is true, conversion is the most natural thing in the world. And because of pluralism, we even might seek to persuade others to see the same truth we know—just as we would if they had a mistaken map of how to find a faraway city. In fact, persuasion is the way we deal with differing views in all other areas of knowledge, such as on the issue of affirmative action, on the best way to deal with the national debt, or on the origins of the American Revolution. We think nothing of debating these issues and trying to persuade or "convert" others to our own viewpoint if we believe the issue to be important enough.

But relativism is offended when people take differences so seriously that they leave one faith to adopt another. According to the relativist, the convert has misunderstood, assuming that the differences are real and substantial when in fact they are not. Relativists claim that the differences cannot be important because nobody really knows anything about who God is or how to approach him.

Relativism, in contrast to pluralism, offers a much more comforting message. Relativism claims that since nobody really knows, we shouldn't worry about the different religious ideas and choices. After all, each road leads to the same place, so we cannot be wrong in any way that matters. It is perfectly safe to ignore God and the questions that he poses.

Pluralism, in contrast, carries the dangerous possibility that since religions are different, some ideas could be right and others wrong. Missing out on the truth could be a very serious matter—we could be accountable to Someone far beyond our sphere of existence or miss out on whole realms of meaning.

From what I've found as I travel and speak in today's universities, relativism is the "opiate of the masses." It deadens and dampens what might otherwise have been the great intellectual and spiritual stimulation and challenge of a truly pluralistic setting. Relativism teaches that the larger questions are out of reach, so why should we worry about them? All that matters is to be happy and sincere, and not to offend others. Students therefore sleepwalk through the most important choices of their lives.

C. S. Lewis touched on the sheer seductiveness of relativism in his description of abandoning his childhood faith. There is a certain comfort in believing that the highest authority to which we will be answerable is our own subjective moral consciousness. He writes,

> I was soon (in the famous words) altering 'I believe' to 'one does feel'. And oh the relief of it! . . . From the tyrannous noon of revelation I passed into the cool evening twilight of Higher Thought, where there was nothing to be obeyed, and nothing to be believed except what was either comforting or exciting.[3]

Relativism may pose as a platform for honest dialogue, but it is more a source of confusion. What we need instead is a respect for honest pluralism and for trying to build an atmosphere of civility as we openly, courageously, and humbly speak about our deepest differences.

Tolerance

Tolerance is living side by side with others with whom we have real and deep differences, but living with respect and civility in our personal attitudes and as much as possible in public policy. Public tolerance for murderers and thieves, for instance, will entail a limited tolerance.

Tolerance is not relativism, nor does it have any necessary relationship to it. A common misconception is that if we question relativism, we must be intolerant and against democracy. But as we have seen, relativism itself is less tolerant than it seems.

We are to be tolerant of people, not necessarily of all their ideas and practices. Tolerance does not demand that we treat any status quo as sacred, as if we were morally obliged to refrain from trying to change ourselves, others, or society. Tolerance does not mean that we never try to persuade someone of the truth of an important idea. It does mean that we hold that person in respect, despite areas of disagreement.

It is true that both tolerant and intolerant people hold to all religious and philosophical persuasions. There are some sad chapters in Christian history, when the people of God have lived out the teaching of their savior poorly. Christians have sometimes been intolerant and prejudiced, as have members of every religion and secular ideology, including relativism.

Once the discussion is on a level playing field—a conversation between two positions that hold differing absolutes—we can move on to the second issue. How does Christ's unique role make sense? Why should there be only one way to God?

WHY ONLY ONE WAY?

Whatever could justify such an outrageous claim as the one made by the early apostles that "There is salvation in no one else, for there is no other name under heaven given among mortals by which we must be saved"? (Acts 4:12) What can make such a counterintuitive idea credible?

As we begin delving into this question, we should realize that Jesus and his followers were not the first to say such things. These exclusive claims began with the monotheism of the Old Testament; that is, they are made of God himself as Creator of heaven and earth (Genesis 1:1). They continue with the insistence on exclusive loyalty and with it the promise of salvation: "Before me no god was formed, nor shall there be any after me. I, I am the LORD, and besides me there is no savior" (Isaiah 43:10–11).

These themes are continued by Jesus and applied to himself. He claimed to transcend time: "Very truly, I tell you, before Abraham was, I am" (John 8:58). More importantly to this discussion, he was seen as the savior of the world. John the Baptist introduced him as ". . . the lamb of God who takes away the sin of the world" (John 1:29).

He saw himself as central to the Father's plan of salvation: ". . . no one knows the Father except the Son and anyone to whom the Son chooses to reveal him. Come to me, all you that are weary and are carrying heavy burdens, and I will give you rest" (Matthew 11:27–28). The early church took these ideas seriously and began their great missionary outreach on the day of Pentecost.

We could consult many theologians who would assure us that the apostles were mistaken and that other, more comfortable ways exist to understand Jesus' claims to uniqueness. But I will begin with a fierce critic of the Christian faith.

Alan Watts was once an Anglican minister who repudiated his faith and turned to his own blend of Eastern religions. In the introduction to his book *Beyond Theology* he relates a turning point in ideas. I will quote him at some length:

> I have previously published three other theological books . . . In varying ways these books attempted a synthesis between traditional Christianity and the unitive mysticism of Hinduism and Buddhism, and in this respect *The Supreme Identity* was probably the most successful. . . .
>
> Upon reflection, this did not satisfy me. There is not a scrap of evidence that the Christian hierarchy was ever aware of itself as one among several lines of transmission for a universal tradition. . . . Any attempt to marry the Vedanta to Christianity must take full account of the fact that Christianity is a contentious faith which requires an all-or-nothing commitment to Jesus as the one and only incarnation of the Son of God. . . .
>
> My previous discussions did not take proper account of that whole aspect of Christianity which is uncompromising, ornery, militant, rigorous, imperious, and invincibly self-righteous. They did not give sufficient weight to the Church's disagreeable insistence on the reality of the totally malignant spirit of cosmic evil, on everlasting damnation, and on the absolute distinction between the Creator and the creature. These thorny and objectionable facets of Christianity cannot be shrugged off as temporary distortions or errors.[4]

Watts brings two important dimensions to our discussion. First is his abandonment of a comfortable relativism under the sheer pressure of the plurality of incompatible teachings. He describes a growing understanding of the irreconcilable differences between religious claims and the dishonesty of trying to homogenize them.

Second is his awareness of the most important places of incompatibility. The Christian faith alone will not fit into his new religion because of three very basic teachings: the creature-Creator distinction, the spirit of totally malignant cosmic evil, and the uniqueness of Christ.

In his hostility to Christianity Watts speaks with far greater clarity than many Christians do about the nature of this division. This is not to say that there are no areas of agreement between the Christian faith and other religions of the world. There certainly are, especially in some areas of ethics.

But when the Christian faith and other worldviews differ on any of these three basic teachings, the differences are not superficial. Let us look at these three points briefly, reversing Watts's order.

The Creature-Creator Distinction

God is Creator, the one who formed and made out of nothing and into nothing. Nothing exists apart from him that he did not create himself. Creation is not a part of him or an extension of his essence; rather he made it separate from himself as a sculptor might make a statue. But God is intimately involved with his creation and with us. His covenant promise was, "I will take you as my people, and I will be your God" (Exodus 6:7). God has revealed himself as a Person—holy, loving, and just.

The divide between Creator and created excludes the idea that we live in a random world in which we are accidents of a mindless, impersonal process that began with one chance event and will end with another. It also excludes the notion that God is the All, and that we in our individuality are like waves on the surface of the vast ocean, having the appearance of individuality for a moment and then merging into the vastness of God. It means that none of us is God nor ever will be.

The creature-Creator distinction also makes possible the Christian teaching that we are created images of God who are not part of him in our essence but who reflect his nature and character. Within all of creation, human beings are distinct in our value and significance. Our lives find their meaning through our relationship to God.

Malignant Cosmic Evil

Goodness is rooted in the character of God himself; he is the source of the moral order in the universe. In opposition to this, evil is real and is a major force in this world. Evil is not a thing or an entity that was created or that has independent existence, but is the way we describe the results of rebellion of God's creatures against God himself. In biblical terms evil is focused in the person of Satan and his influence on earth.

Evil is rooted in human sin, which is not misfortune or hardship but a betrayal, a covenant-breaking treason. It is the human being refusing to be a creature and somehow wanting to displace God and his authority. It is essentially moral in its nature.

· Evil is responsible for human destructiveness in its many variations—from the moral monsters of our race such as Hitler, Stalin, and Pol Pot to the much more respectable meanness and selfishness that characterize ordinary people. As a rebellion aimed first against God, it then trickles down in a process of near infinite complexity into all of life. The biblical bad news is that all people will one day have to face their Creator in a final accountability and will ultimately be found without excuse.

This view of evil separates the Christian from many other religions and worldviews. It excludes Alan Watts's notion that since everything is God, good and evil are equally part of him. And it is incompatible with the idea behind William Blake's poem, "The Marriage of Heaven and Hell," which was the reason behind C. S. Lewis writing *The Great Divorce*. In answering Blake, Lewis argued that good and evil are finally separated, never having been married.

If the Christian view of evil is true, many other beliefs about evil are not, including those that minimize evil by locating it only in some aspect of the self or society. For instance, a Marxist might see it in private ownership of industry, a feminist might find it in the patriarchal system, and the average American in inadequate education, economic inequality, or low self-esteem. These many minimized views of evil come with the promise that evil, like a well-trained dog, can be brought to heal when the particular problem area is corrected.

This may seem to be the "down side" of the Christian faith, but like nothing else it opens doors of understanding that enable us to make sense of our moral life. It means that our feelings of guilt are not intrinsically illusory and misleading but are sometimes clues to real moral problems. It also means that our feelings of moral outrage (at Hitler, Stalin, and Pol Pot, for example) are not necessarily just empty self-righteousness, but could be valid or even necessary moral responses to the violation of a real moral order.

As Blaise Pascal, the seventeenth-century French mathematician and apologist, wrote about original sin, "Certainly nothing jolts us more rudely than this doctrine, and yet, but for the mystery, the most incomprehensible of all, we remain incomprehensible to ourselves."[5]

The Solution in Jesus Christ

Into this world and the moral predicament caused by sin and evil comes the solution through Jesus of Nazareth. His coming, ministry, death, and resurrection can be understood only in terms of the biblical diagnosis of the deepest human problem—a moral alienation from God resulting from human sin.

Although his teaching and life give an example of how we should live, this was not the only reason for his coming, nor would it have made him the unique source of salvation. High moral teaching and good example are wonderfully instructive, but they do not help those who have already broken the law and stand liable for punishment. If convicted criminals await punishment, it is not "good news" to read them the law or to offer them an example of law-keeping.

This is why Jesus came to accomplish for us what we could not do for ourselves without being destroyed. He came to die on the cross to bear the full and complete punishment for the sins of all those who would trust in him, the penalty they would otherwise have had to pay themselves. He stood in our place, under the judgment of God as he died, that we might be free from the liability for our own sin. No amount of teaching or example could have done this for us.

The message of Jesus is rightfully called the "gospel," or "good news," because salvation from the just judgment of God is promised to all those who sincerely ask for it. It is granted freely without the merit of the one who receives it. Those forgiven are adopted into the family of God and are helped by the Holy Spirit to follow the teaching and example of Jesus.

It was not Jesus' claim to divinity alone that made him unique. Hinduism, for example, has many incarnations of divinity called "avatars." Nor do his moral teaching and example so set him apart. Rather his uniqueness lies in his coming to do what only God could have done, to provide a sufficient sacrificial payment for human sin. The major human figures in both the Old Testament and the New Testament, the prophet Moses and the apostle Paul, both would have given their lives for the sake of the people, but their offers were ignored by God.

The biblical diagnosis of the human condition is that we cannot do anything to save ourselves. In fact our attempts to save ourselves without relying on God's grace further express the very rebellion at the heart of the problem—our refusal to admit our brokenness. We can be saved only by grace because we are helplessly enmeshed in sin.

The solution to the human predicament had to be so radical because the predicament was so serious. No one in Jesus' time or our own has wanted to believe that we need so much help. Certainly his own disciples did not. The solution, rooted in God's great love for us, had to be that God himself would come in human form and die a sacrificial death.

THE IMPORTANCE OF THE DIAGNOSIS

The key to understanding our question, "why only one way?" depends entirely on our ability to understand and accept the diagnosis of the human condition for which Jesus provides the cure. If we do not grasp the depth of human sin, then the Christian insistence on "Christ alone" will seem weird and arbitrary, originating in Christian insecurity, not moral necessity. In fact it has nothing to do with Christian insecurity and everything to do with moral necessity.

I once spoke to a man who told me angrily, "I didn't ask Jesus to die for me. I think that's highly manipulative!" I realized that he was absolutely right—unless sin is a serious problem. If I were to offer to die for you because of my love for you, let's say by jumping in front of a truck on your behalf, what would you think? What would it do for you? It might mean that you would need therapy for post-traumatic stress disorder! Of course it would be entirely different if my dying actually gave you some enormous benefit, fulfilling some desperate need. Otherwise the giving up of one's life for another is a bizarre, neurotic gesture.

So it is with Jesus. For those who do not realize or acknowledge their need, the salvation he offers seems irrelevant, superfluous, and manipulative. He is a savior in midair, come to save when nobody needs saving and yet asking for total commitment. The Christian must sympathize with those who have trouble seeing that Christ is a unique savior; to the modern mind, the idea is truly outrageous. We must try to explain the context in which his salvation makes overwhelming sense.

The existence of sin and therefore the need for such a radical solution is the only explanation for the otherwise outrageous claim that Jesus is the only way to God. The exclusiveness of the Christian faith rests on the cross, without which no one would be saved from the consequences of their sin. The idea of the cross in turn rests on the reality of sin, without which it would have been unnecessary. Unless sin is an overwhelmingly serious problem, Jesus is a superfluous savior.

So we must then shift the discussion one step back to the question of what really is the true human condition. At this point it is the Christian who has some very pointed questions to ask in the modern world. Who has the most realistic assessment of human nature? Is it not conceivable that human evil is such a serious and pervasive a problem? If we ourselves get angry and indignant about outrageous injustice and moral evil done in the world, won't God also be indignant and angry? Is it likely that God is less morally sensitive than we are?

A CONCLUDING CHALLENGE

The uniqueness of Christ is not a peripheral teaching of the Christian faith. If we lose our sense of absolute dependence on what Jesus did, it will erode away the whole of the faith until little remains. But equally important to holding to the uniqueness of Christ is not acting arrogant or superior to those who do not agree or who are not Christians. Nothing so quickly discredits this biblical claim than if we make it without love, or in pride, defensiveness, conceit, or if we refuse to discuss it at all.

In our society many people begin with the assumption that the only reason to make such an outrageous claim is if one is arrogant, ignorant, or both. If the Christian *is* arrogant in discussion and personal demeanor, then he or she has just walked, flat-footed, into the non-Christian stereotype. We will seem to have proven the non-Christian's point, and we will have enabled them to dismiss the claims of Christ with a more peaceful mind.

This introduces the important issue that part of the persuasiveness of the Christian faith includes factors that are not, strictly speaking, cognitive—a point too often neglected in discussions of apologetics. It raises the matter of who we are as we try to defend the truth of God and persuade others. What looms large is our own character, the quality of our love, and our ability to relate to other people with both courage and sensitivity.

A closely related factor is the Christian community—where Christian people as they live and relate to each other can demonstrate something of the truth of God. Francis Schaeffer wrote that the love and sense of community between Christians is the "final apologetic." But for the Christian community to function in this way, it must not be a tribal community. It is to that challenge that we now turn.

6

The Church as Community

WE HAVE SEEN THE WAY a recovery of apologetics can protect us against both sides of our polarization. On the one hand, apologetics maintains a Christian awareness of the surrounding culture and how to challenge its ideas and loyalties, which protects against chameleon-style accommodation. And on the other hand, because of its nature as being challenging and persuading, apologetics also removes much of the fear of contact with the non-Christian world that fuels tribalism and gives the musk-ox option its seductive attraction.

So also community is another pressure point for salt and light that cuts against both chameleon and musk ox. Community is necessary for helping people resist becoming chameleons. So often Christians turn into chameleons from being too alone: Having no other people of like mind near them, they gradually start to think that their dissonant beliefs are crazy and so began to blend in. An isolated individual is too weak to stand or to maintain perspective. We need the support and accountability of others, not just for our own Christian survival but to be salt and light into our society.

How does community help us against the musk ox, tribal side of the polarity? Some might say that the musk-ox problem is one of having too much community. If so, then the solution would be self-sufficient, isolated, Christian individualists—a basic contradiction in terms. The problem with tribalism is not

87

that the strength of community is too great. Rather it is that the nature of the community is skewed in an ingrown direction.

The church as community must provide the support and accountability that we need and God commands. But that involves offering an alternative to tribalism. That is, the church must be a community that leads, equips, and encourages its members to reach out into the surrounding society. It will face both inward and outward.

Actually, there is no necessary connection between the existence of community and tribalism. Of course there are tribal communities, but there are also communities that are not tribal. Then there are far too many Christian groups and churches that have a full tribal set of attitudes and commitments but have no sense of community at all—the worst of both worlds.

CHANGING INTIMACIES

We will begin with the idea of community itself. The creation of community is an enormous challenge, especially since, in order to exist, it must push back the many fragmenting and individualistic forces in modern society. My main focus in this chapter will be on the church as community, but most of what I say applies to other groups of Christians as well. Any notion of community must be flexible enough to relate to many different situations and combinations of people.

For example, think of Jesus himself. His best friend seems to have been John and his two other closest friends were Peter and James. He also had twelve disciples who traveled with him during his three-year ministry, the seventy who were commissioned to take the gospel to the towns of Palestine, and the one hundred twenty who were in the upper room together after his death. There were also others, not necessarily included in these numbers, who seemed to travel with the twelve some of the time.

As we can see, Jesus had different kinds of relationships with different people. We do too, and those with whom we associate and are intimate will change in the various stages of our lives. In the midst of this diversity, what does the word "community" mean?

WHAT IT IS NOT

It's best to begin the exploration by outlining two things I do *not* mean by "Christian community." One is that it is not a God-substitute. When the idea of community is in vogue, people tend to use it as a subtle replacement for God. They derive meaning from their involvement with a community, whether church-related or not, instead of from God himself. But real community among Christians happens only when individuals living under the lordship of Christ commit themselves to each other.

The other is that Christian community is not a "lifestyle enclave." Sociologist Robert Bellah and his colleagues use this term in their book, *Habits of the Heart*, to describe what often counterfeits community in modern America. Lifestyle enclaves are groupings of people who spend time together around some aspect of their lifestyle, such as playing bridge, poker, or golf, tasting wine, stock-car racing, collecting art, or watching professional sports on television.

Unlike community, a lifestyle enclave is restricted in two senses: It has to do with private life or leisure time, not public life, and it is restricted to those who share some aspect of one's lifestyle. In Bellah's words, it "celebrates the narcissism of similarity."[1] Very little is necessarily common in the worldviews of the participants and relatively little is necessarily shared of the full scope of life. The paradigm would be the club.

Lifestyle enclaves are often mistaken for community today. Sadly, much of what happens in the life of churches and Christian groups is solidly within the limitations of a church club or lifestyle enclave. Both liberal and conservative churches are at risk. The larger the church, the greater the risk.

AN UNNATURAL UNITY

So what is Christian community? In its most basic form, it is a group of Christians who honor God by the way they interact with each other. Sharing a worldview and sense of ultimate loyalty to Christ, they have in common basic ideas about the sort of world we live in. They would have shared notions of how we came to exist, who we are as human beings, what are our deepest problems and the ultimate solutions, and which hopes are worth pursuing.

Members are committed to Jesus as the Lord and thus meet together to celebrate biblical truths and to teach, to participate in the sacraments, encourage, and strengthen each other. They are accountable to one other and share significant time together, not just a few minutes after a church service over coffee.

Christian communities must be both inward and outward looking: While members use their vast diversity of gifts to serve each other they also are involved in public life in their locality, caring for and sharing the gospel of Christ with their neighbors.

Christian community is an unnatural unity, unlike a lifestyle enclave in which a shared interest brings people together. The New Testament church was anything but a homogeneous group. It was made up of Jews and Gentiles, young and old, slaves and slave owners, male and female. It had a host of characters from ex-prostitutes, ex-priests, and ex-practitioners of magic to fishermen, zealots (the terrorists of the first century), and tax collectors (collaborators with the Roman establishment).

Theirs was a far greater ethnic, economic, political, and social diversity than we have in America today. Yet their love for and commitment to each other each other made some of the Romans call them "the third race." Never before were divisions between people bridged so dramatically. The early Christians were not without problems and conflicts, but their life together gave powerful credibility to their faith and the truth of their message.

REFLECTIONS OF TRANSCENDENCE

Community is important because the word as I am using it is simply short-hand for God's commands about how we relate to each other. It is impossible to obey Jesus' commands to love without building community.

Love is not just for the lovely or for those easy to love because they will love you back; love continues even if we tire of the person and want to move on. As the first letter of John says, we shouldn't fool ourselves into thinking that we love God whom we cannot see if we do not love the brothers and sisters whom we can (1 John 4:20).

Christian community involves loving the least of the followers of Christ, for in doing so we are loving Christ. To grasp this stretches our imagination enormously. But we also have Paul's stern warning that if we do not love, we are nothing, gain nothing, but are just making noise (1 Corinthians 13:1–3).

Community is important in the life of the church not only because God commands it but because the life of the church depends on it. In a fragmented world that exalts transience and has little time for anything permanent, what institution will stand for values that are both permanent and life-giving? What body will provide the setting for us to experience these truths and pass them on to our children? How can the church be such a necessary and vital social force today if it is hollowed out interpersonally?

The church as community also provides a living statement of God's truth to the world. It incarnates the truth that we are all one as creatures of the Creator God, made in his image, and of great value to him. It shows that we are all one as sinners, enmeshed in our brokenness and rebellion against God, ourselves, and one another. And it reveals the people of God as one in Christ, redeemed by the rescue operation of God. The Holy Spirit unifies the church at all of these levels.

MARKS OF CHRISTIAN COMMUNITY

What characteristics of community should we, with the help of God, be aiming for? There are many, but four in particular stand out.

The first is that the Christian church must be a community of grace. God's grace is not to be only a doctrine we believe in our hearts and minds and confess in our liturgies, but something that we act out by the way we treat people. One of the great catastrophes is that Christians have allowed the population at large to associate faith with people who give the appearance of having been morally upright from birth. Too often being a Christian appears to mean being squeaky clean, always respectable, well-dressed—and usually without much joy.

This is a tragedy because the church is meant for bent and broken sinners, people who have acknowledged their failures in the most important areas of life. It is true that we are dedicated to moral and spiritual transformation with the help of God, but the entrance to the church is through honesty about where we have gone wrong and an acknowledgment of our need for God's mercy. The church cannot afford to have many people pretending not to need grace, and still have any sense of community.

Dietrich Bonhoeffer in his wonderful book *Life Together* warned of the danger of living in a dreamworld of naive ideas about community. He wrote,

> . . . God desires to lead us to a knowledge of genuine Christian fellowship, so surely must we be overwhelmed by a great general disillusionment with others, with Christians in general, and, if we are fortunate, with ourselves.[2]

With these attitudes solidly in place we can have a community of grace. Our hope will not be in our own achievements or moral character but in the mercy of God to us.

The second characteristic of community is that love reaches into the whole of life and crosses natural boundaries between people of different race, culture, economic class, sex, and age.

On Pentecost, the birthday of the church, many nations were represented when Peter saw the fulfillment of the prophecy of Joel. This prophet had declared that the Spirit of God would be poured out on all flesh: sons and daughters, young and old, men and women, slaves and free. The joyous proclamation was that Christ would relativize all divisions—age, race, class, and gender.

Those in the early church loved with their hearts and their material goods. They freely gave to each other, sharing possessions beyond an easy sense of comfort. This love included hospitality, as advised by the apostle Peter: "Be hospitable to one another without complaining" (1 Peter 4:9). All of this is not likely to increase the resale value of our houses—if we own them—or of the furniture in them. Yet what an impact it can have in a society where everybody's home is their castle, a citadel of private life.

The third distinctive feature of the church as a community is a commitment to its place of geographical location. What we strive for in building community is more realistic the closer people live to each other geographically. With the loss of the natural interdependence of village life this is difficult but not impossible.

A Christian church should be concerned with the well-being of its particular location, such as working on the local social, economic, and environmental challenges. The problems of the people who live near us will be our own. The church should not become a political pressure group but it ought to encourage the people of God to be involved responsibly outside the walls of the church.

A fourth mark of community is a commitment to reconciliation. By this I do not mean burying grievances beneath long-term resentments or splitting up in order to escape the conflict. Nor do I mean resisting the illusion that we will never have conflict because we are all mature Christians.

The word of God gives us three tools for reconciliation: confession, forgiveness, and reproof. Each is important for building true community. The first, confession, is simply being honest enough to admit our own sin to those whom we have sinned against. We must admit it not just in general or to God only, but specifically to the one offended. This means that confession is not a long list of excuses or explanations but a simple asking of forgiveness for having committed the wrong.

Forgiveness is canceling the debt of another person's sin against us. Jesus calls us to forgive not just little sins, but even those that are serious, painful, and inexcusable. We do not need to say we are no longer hurt, or that we can trust again the one who has hurt us (sometimes a very foolish idea). Instead, forgiveness is letting a matter drop, not holding it over another's head, canceling the emotional and moral debt. When we refuse to forgive we endanger our relationship with God and wreck the church community.

Reproof is telling another that he or she is doing something wrong. Some people find it much too hard to do; others find it much too easy. Whatever our temperament, at times we will be obligated to tell others of their sin. Otherwise, through cruelty or fear of rejection, we can consign them to that sin.

God has given us these tools for resolving conflict because he recognizes that we will need to use them. If the church employs them consistently and well, few conflicts need divide the people of God seriously.

FROM CHAOS TO COMMUNITY

How, then, is community built? What are some of the steps? These are difficult questions because many different levels of relationship and commitment exist at one time in a church. But psychiatrist M. Scott Peck's experiences in trying to build community can be instructive.

Peck worked mainly in weekend workshops with people who had not known each other before but who came together for the purpose of experiencing community. The settings were therefore artificial, making their application to church life questionable. I suspect, however, that some of the dynamics he charts will ring true to church members. Here is a summary of his findings about the stages that groups go through in working toward community.[3]

The beginning stage is usually what he calls "pseudo-community." This is a time of etiquette and good manners. Everyone exercises their social skills and tries to show how much they have in common with each other and how glad they are to be together, keeping carefully to generalities.

The second stage moving toward community is "chaos." Pseudo-community soon wears thin if people spend any time with each other. They begin to confront their differences and insecurities and begin to try to control, convert, or heal each other. When they are unsuccessful, they argue about why community is not taking place and whose fault it is. Differences are no longer hidden. Everybody is trying to obliterate them by changing others to be as normal as they are.

The third stage is "emptiness." Peck writes that this is not a stage of Buddhist spirituality but rather a time when people relinquish the need to control, convert, or heal each other. They empty themselves of their prejudices, preconceptions, and the need to fix each other. Peck sees the desire to convert or fix others as a self-centered urge to control without making the costly effort to listen and understand. In the Christian view, this emptying is simply a confrontation with personal sin and selfishness—a collective realization of brokenness and failure.

The final stage is, of course, "community." Now communication happens that involves really listening to each other with empathy and understanding. Differences are accepted and people are no longer seen as projects. At this point, ironically, healing and conversion can actually happen. Community here is not some new interpersonal reality or social structure, but people treating each other as the valuable human beings that they are.

We must understand that these four stages form an observed sequence in largely artificial settings. In a church these stages are all going on simultaneously, or parts of a church might go back and forth between them at various times. But Peck's analysis gives a useful description of the struggles we face in realizing a community of grace, love, and reconciliation.

MODERN OBSTACLES

What stands in the way of building community? The most important obstacle is that it is just too hard. It demands too much sacrifice, too much of one's security, freedom, time, and resources. But Christian people have always experienced some form of the tension between individual freedom and community. The modern industrialized world, however, presents some new obstacles.

"Modernity" is the word usually applied to the vast complex of changes that have come on us from the Industrial Revolution. Robert Reich, professor of political economy at Harvard, puts the picture in an abbreviated form:

> Most Americans no longer live in traditional communities. They live in suburban subdivisions bordered by highways and sprinkled with shopping malls, or in tony condominiums and residential clusters, or in ramshackle apartment buildings and housing projects. Most of them commute to work and socialize on some basis other than geographic proximity. And most people pick up and move to a different neighborhood every five years or so.[4]

We could add to this list great changes in mobility, transportation, science, technology of all sorts, medicine, communications, education, and the application of technique to all areas of life. Each development is double-edged, having an obvious benefit for which it was designed as well as consequences that were unintended, direct and indirect, helpful and harmful.

Having noted some of the negative consequences of modernity for the individual, church, and family, we need to think critically about how to lean against these challenges in imaginative ways. I will mention three specific points that can and should be resisted.

Like Attracts Like

The first is homogeneity. The modern world works most smoothly when people come together who are just like each other. In countless settings avoiding others' differences seems easiest and most efficient. Advertisers, for instance, key in on their target audience in terms of age, sex, income, and education.

But it is a mistake to assume that the church of Christ, in the name of efficiency or effectiveness, should aim at homogeneity. What works in marketing may actually destroy the church and turn it into a lifestyle enclave. Seeking for people who are all alike implies that the apostle Paul got it wrong when he suggested that the church's strength was in its internal diversity.[5] It is also a far cry from the church in its completed form, created "from every tribe and language and people and nation" (Revelation 5:9).

Another aspect of the shift to homogeneity is the mistake of welcoming segregation by age. Division of the adult from the young, and the young from each other by age, has only been the norm since work was removed from the home and the public-school system established. The result has been a great number of young people only having close relationships in their peer group. Adults are usually known only in some official capacity.

This development is new in social history and is not positive. It means that young people are isolated from the very people who could be guides, mentors, models, and friends. Also, older children are not given the responsibility to spend time with and care for younger children. This pattern deprives the young person of positive identification with the adult world. It makes the transition to adulthood a leap into the unknown.

Much of the church has embraced this change. Different church groups exist for each age category, with larger churches having a stricter and more fine-tuned segregation. These divisions are then continued with college groups, graduate-student groups, married and singles groups, divorced groups, and so on.

Not all age divisions are wrong; obvious advantages flow from being able to meet specific needs. But the church is ideally equipped to mix ages also, by arranging activities that involve people from a wide age range. Social-service projects, for example, provide wonderful opportunities for this.

On the Move

The second point of resistance to modernity concerns the issue of mobility. In American society, the economic system gets the first choice of one's gifts, abilities, and career. If Christians are part of the individualist American dream they are likely to be enslaved to this system.

Thus many adults now move every three to five years, whenever an old or new employer demands it. They uproot themselves and their families from schools, churches, other neighbors, extended families, and local areas in answering the call of upward mobility.

How can our gifts be available to the church if we follow this way of life? For most people it probably takes several years in a church before they know others well enough for their gifts to be used fruitfully. Of course mobility is not wrong per se; sometimes the only jobs we can get require us to change locations, and sometimes moving is clearly right.

But having said that, I suspect Christians often need to resist the pressure of mobility for the sake of community in family and church.

Professionals and Professionalism

The third place for resistance is professionalism in Christian leadership, an issue with many sides. First of all, by resisting professionalism I do not mean resisting competence or specialized training. Professionalism in the negative sense can be an attitude of the clergy and of the congregation. For the congregation it means that the minister or ministerial staff are the people paid to make the church happen. They are the ones to do the Christian work and be the "spiritual" people. The rest of the congregation doesn't really have the time or expertise. This may well "work smoothly," but it entirely undercuts both the nature of the church as the body of Christ and the spiritual stature of its members as the priesthood of all believers.

Then there is the professional attitude of the clergy. Often this means seeing the ministry in terms of techniques of communication, administration, demography, fund-raising, and the ability to project the CEO/therapist image. The result is the sort of distance between minister and congregation suggested by the letter writing that we spoke of in chapter 2.

The building of the church as community has never been easy. It must stand against the force of human selfishness and many isolating social forces. Pre-industrial times had certain social and economic incentives to community that no longer are part of the picture. Yet the building of community has not become less important, just more difficult.

COMMUNITY AS SALT AND LIGHT

Lastly, let us look at theological perspectives in three critical areas that either help or hinder the working of salt and light in the Christian community.

Disagreement but Respect

Abraham once lived in Gerar where he knew that there was "no fear of God at all in this place, and they will kill me because of my wife" (Genesis 20:11). So clear was this conviction that, in order to save his own life, he gave his wife Sarah to the king to marry. God intervened, however, and the king ended up rebuking Abraham.

Is it possible that Christians today make similar mistakes about our godless culture? Knowing how to live in a society that is predominantly not Christian is a humbling challenge. On the one hand we can be naive about evil, but on the other we can be condescending from a place of supposed moral superiority. Two examples illustrate.

In 1970 Francis Schaeffer wrote that one of the most vital priorities for the Christian church would be to learn how to be co-belligerents with the world without being allies with it.[6] By this he meant that Christians would have to learn to engage in social, political, and cultural causes alongside non-Christian people with whom they would disagree on other issues.

We must understand issues not in packages, but one at a time. As we work together with some people on one issue, we know that we might work against them on other issues. Unless we can learn to keep this tension, our pessimism and censoriousness will lead us to be marginalized as lonely voices outside the culture, or we will be swept along by our undiscerning optimism in the flow of accommodation.

Too many Christians have such a negative attitude toward the society around them that they never could work closely with anyone but fellow members of the tribe. When society starts to come unraveled around them they say with satisfaction, "There, I told you so. You can't live without God."

This is a failure of opportunity, love, and service. As we look at history, we can see many points at which Christian people have, with God's help, made significant contributions in almost every area of endeavor.

The second illustration regards Tim Keller, a minister who has started an extremely fruitful church ministry in one of the world centers of secularism, New York City. He gives intriguing advice to others thinking of such a challenge:

> It is not enough to simply pity the city and the people you are trying to serve, but you must embrace it, expect to learn and be taught by it. You need to respect and love the people you are trying to reach, not just feel sorry for them. The minister must be energized by the city, not simply drained by it (though it will have a draining aspect). This positive view of the city and love for it will come through to the people you are trying to reach. Without it, you will only attract others who are in the city temporarily. Without it, the people you are trying to reach will feel they are being "talked down to."

There is a need for a good understanding of the opportunities and strengths of the city—a Biblical Theology of the city. You are not a church in the city, but a church for the city.[7]

Keller is certainly not naive about the forces of evil in the city. But he realizes that if God is at work there, we must start with a positive sense of his activity and presence and of people living there who are made in his image.

A Place for Women

There must be a careful rethinking of the place of women in evangelical churches. The dangers are, predictably, in both directions. Some have thrown away the authority of the Bible in order to adapt as chameleons to feminist theories. Others have followed the tribal musk ox and are threatened by the very word "feminism."

The New Testament shows women in church leadership as prophets and as co-workers in the gospel with the apostle Paul, and Junia probably was an apostle (Romans 16:7). In the Old Testament as far back as the Book of Judges, Deborah had the highest religious and political position in the nation. There is no indication that this was some sort of exception that broke the rules, nor was it treated as a humorous anomaly.

Yet many evangelical churches today that hold a high view of the Bible do not allow women to pass the offering plate. They have gone backward from the Book of Judges. If a modern-day Deborah were to come to church, what would she do with her gifts?

I realize that the question of women's eldership is a controversial one, given two Pauline passages.[8] But those who believe that women are not permitted to be elders can still do a great deal more than is often allowed for women to express their gifts according to the wider biblical pattern.

This issue has everything to do with the nature of the Christian community that a church can be. Women make up, after all, more than half the population of most churches.

Our Language

The Bible tells us that "Death and life are in the power of the tongue" (Proverbs 18:21). As Christians we are wise to take account of the enormous importance of language, particularly in our own contemporary cultural setting.

Our language can brand us in public as soon as we open our mouths. If we speak in tribal Christian clichés, we stereotype ourselves as those who are culturally strange and living in a private world. It becomes far easier to dismiss us and all that we stand for.

C. S. Lewis was one of the most effective communicators of the gospel during his own lifetime and remains so even now, over thirty years after his death. One reason is that he kept his vocabulary free from all the typically religious words, terms, and idioms. He labored to express his faith in fresh, nonreligious terms.

If we can follow Lewis in this way, people will not sense that they are hearing something archaic, but rather something alive, deeply human, and challenging. Although our language may seem to be a small matter, it will have a lot to do with whether our community can relate to those outside the tribe.

As we have seen in this chapter, as our society drifts toward greater fragmentation and as real and open community becomes increasingly rare, the importance of the community issue will increase. If Christians cannot produce living communities, they will be seen to have failed to provide what people need, just as the secular world has failed. The name of God will again be scoffed at as powerless to engage modern problems of isolation.

But if Christians can honor God by the way they live in community they can be a powerful, persuasive force for the truth of the gospel. As the apostle Paul said in writing to the church in Corinth, "You yourselves are our letter, written on our hearts, to be known and read by all" (2 Corinthians 3:2). Although community is a challenge that seems beyond us, it is the task that Jesus himself has given us, promising not to leave us.

7

Returning to the Foundations

THE UNHAPPY POLARIZATION and weakening of the church that we have been exploring has produced what is often called an evangelical crisis of identity. Evangelical churches have been pulled in both the chameleon and musk-ox directions. Their failure to be salt and light has undermined their effectiveness in every aspect of service to God.

Lamin Sanneh, a scholar of missions and world Christianity, has described the same problem in slightly different terms. He sees three historical attitudes of the church to culture. One is *accommodation*, where attitudes of compromise predominate over those of faithfulness and resistance—what we have called the chameleon. Another is the opposite response, that of *quarantine* in which attitudes of self-sufficiency, isolation, and defiance are characteristic—what we have named musk-ox tribalism.

Sanneh's third view is *prophetic reform*, the attitude "in which critical selectiveness determines the attitude toward the world."[1] This view neither embraces the world uncritically nor rejects it blindly. Instead it is the attitude of salt and light, of being in the world but not of it. It will engage the world prophetically; that is, it will challenge the world not from a narrow tribalism that is timid or defiant but from a position that is thoughtful and supported with prayer over chosen issues and events.

In the third option, prophetic reform, Christian truth is neither compromised nor confined but is put to work to sustain the church and ultimately to transform individuals and society at large. This is the real identity of the church of Christ.

Jesus himself takes this approach when he speaks about salt and light in the Sermon on the Mount. He says, "Let your light shine before others, so that they may see your good works and give glory to your Father in heaven" (Matthew 5:16). The qualities of salt and light make an impact on the world outside the church.

The only way to be in a prophetic role under God's direction is to listen to God first. We are not called to trust our own moral intuitions and sensibilities nor the winds of current moral fashions. Instead we must let the word of God be prophetic to us, in us, and for us.

The most obvious way to let God speak to us is through the Bible itself. One of the most enlightening images used of the Scriptures is the word of God as a "two-edged sword." This term occurs in Hebrews 4:12, Revelation 1:16, and Revelation 2:12 and refers to the Roman executioner's sword. Its meaning is suggested in the apostle John's use of the term in the passage that follows, the letters to the seven churches in Revelation 2–3.

The word as a sword refers not first the word's ability to give comfort but rather to be painfully prophetic in its cutting away what should not be there and killing what should not have life. The two edges may be seen at least metaphorically to represent the two directions of that prophetic word. In the letters to the seven churches, the sword cut out into the ideas and practices of the world to challenge and reform them, especially when those ideas worked their way into the church. But the sword of the word reached in another direction also, cutting back into the life, habits, and practices of the church that needed reform.

THE SWORD'S FRONT EDGE

Look first at the front edge of the sword of God's word in the letters to the seven churches. Take, for example, the church at Pergamum (Revelation 2:12–17). Jesus began by commending them for the courage of their stand against persecution. One of their members had been martyred when he refused to deny his faith in Christ. When faced with a clear threat, he had stood in faith to his death.

But Jesus then moved to his concern that the church was starting to turn in a chameleon direction. He saw that instead of confronting and exposing heretical teaching that had come from the outside, they had been accepting of it. The risen Christ mentioned two issues, the teaching of Balaam and the teaching of the Nicolaitans.

The teaching of Balaam seems particularly important.[2] Balaam was a prophet who was hired by a Moabite king, Balak, to destroy the Israelites by cursing them. But God was committed to the Israelites by covenant so Balaam's curses each time turned into blessings—much to the frustration of Balak who had paid good money for a curse. The king and his prophet were unsuccessful in their direct attempts to destroy Israel.

Later, however, Balaam advised a different strategy.[3] He realized that the Israelites were protected by God when they stood in faith, so it was impossible to overpower that protection. But if one could corrupt their faith and lead them to follow idols and immoral ways of living, then God would turn and judge them himself. Balaam's teaching seemed to be that of encouraging believers in the true God to follow idols—that is, to be chameleons. This was probably the connection to the Nicolaitans, who some scholars think were precursors of later Gnostic groups. The Nicolaitans seemed to draw Christians into sexual promiscuity and tolerance of idolatry.

In his letter Jesus confronted this chameleon tendency in the church. It had not just slowed their outreach to their neighbors; it had so diluted their critical selectiveness that it was in danger of corrupting the church itself.

We see the same front edge of the sword of the word of God in Jesus' words to the church in Thyatira in Revelation 2:20. Instead of confronting the prophetess Jezebel, the church in Thyatira tolerated her idolatry and immorality. Too easily this church had soaked up pagan ideas and practices, becoming far too resonant with the surrounding culture. And so again the word of God challenged saltless salt, the chameleon pattern.

What we see in Jesus' letters is a call for theological clarity and a spiritually informed view of one's society's ideas and practices. We may not be threatened by Nicolaitans or Jezebel today, but we have our own equivalent forms of unbelief that have been left unchallenged and have made their way into the church.

This raises a key point. The front edge of the word of God must be kept sharp in each generation against the forces that dull it and allow God's people to become more resonant with current accepted wisdom.

It is not enough to be experts on the early church, the Reformation, Puritans, or the Enlightenment if we are clueless about our own day. We need to understand and confront idolatry, injustice, and unbelief where it is most important in our own world.

THE SWORD'S BACK EDGE

The second edge of the sword is the word of God striking back into the church against all its introversions, sacred cows, and traditions that have no biblical warrant. It challenges musk-ox tribalism.

We can see this side of the sword being wielded in Jesus' letter to the church in Ephesus in Revelation 2:1–7. This church had stood against the Nicolaitans and had been attentive to the need for clear theological definition, carefully testing out whether those who claimed to be apostles were true or false. They had endured suffering patiently.

But Jesus was concerned because they had lost their first love. Perhaps they had become hard and insensitive in their defense of orthodoxy, for when a group focuses only on doctrinal purity, that preoccupation can produce isolation. Or perhaps they had a self-satisfaction or self-righteousness that made it hard to notice the challenges of love surrounding them.

Another example of the back edge of the sword of God's word can be seen in Jesus' letter to the church in Sardis in Revelation 3:1–5. In this letter we can easily see contemporary parallels. For instance, Jesus wrote, "You have a name of being alive, but you are dead" (Revelation 3:1). A telltale sign of tribalism is the tendency to live off a reputation earned in the past. The church in Sardis had been a church with great vitality but now they were a church of precious nostalgia, kept only marginally alive by their memories of faith in an earlier time.

Both the church in Ephesus and the church in Sardis betray strong tribal influences. They have become blind to Christ's vision for them to be lights to the world in their present moment. But God's word, as a sharp two-edged sword, lays these bare.

So too today—if we let the back edge of God's word get dull, we gratify all the tribal urges and temptations for security on earth with their fear of fresh perspectives and reform. By doing so we allow the church to remove itself from the world and retreat into obscurantism and self-corruption. No light shines out.

But when the back edge is sharp, the church can recover and be reformed from the rubble of compromise and corruption. Think, for instance, of how compromised the church in the United States has been on the issue of race relations. Without the dynamic of the back edge of God's sword cutting into the church from the Abolition movement in the first half of the nineteenth century and the civil-rights movement over a hundred years later, a great proportion of the church might still be standing against the truth of God on the issue of race. American society at large also would have lacked that prophetic influence that began in the church but then ended slavery nationally, and has at last begun to undo the racial injustice of so many centuries.

G. K. Chesterton wrote that as he observed the history of the church, "At least five times the Faith has gone to the dogs. In each of these five cases, it was the dog that died."[4] What Chesterton observed here was that throughout its history the church of Christ has shown a moral and spiritual resilience. At times it has sunk to terrible defeat, corruption, and scandal. But the church has been given the Holy Spirit and the word of God. Where there has been humility and openness to self-criticism there has been repentance and reform. And where there has been repentance and reform, the church has regained its life and the surrounding society has felt the benefit in social transformation.

Christ's warnings to the churches in Asia Minor are very serious. He told several of the churches that their status as true churches of Christ might be removed. In fact, the cities where the churches were most severely rebuked—Sardis and Laodicea—exist today only as ruins.

GOD HAS NOT GIVEN UP

In the letters to the seven churches we can see the prophetic power of the word of God as it cuts through what should not be there. But this prophetic reproof is not the only function of the word of God; nor is it the only theme in these letters. The word from the risen Christ carries profound comfort and hope as well.

He knew of the churches' distress and patience in suffering; of those who had paid the ultimate price in the rising persecution; of those who had suffered in poverty; of their failure, their faithfulness, their good works. Jesus knew of their tribulation and also of their successes and victories. Nothing escaped him. And from what he saw, he encouraged them to grow in faith, hope, and love.

Another major part of his message was that—despite his rebukes—the basic promises of Christian hope still hold. Words of victory appear often. To the one who conquered in faith over the trials and difficulties in this world he promised the tree of life (Revelation 2:7), one's name written in the book of life (Revelation 3:5), escape from the second death (Revelation 2:11), and ultimately to rule with him from his throne (Revelation 3:21).

A church or Christian group that acts as salt and light and holds an attitude of prophetic reform cannot look to the world for its ultimate security. Our source of safety lies neither in being comfortably accepted by the world nor in being smugly isolated from it. In fact, the common flaw in both sides of the polarization is ultimately the same—a worldliness that seeks security from this world more than from God himself. If the two edges of the word of God work in our individual lives and in our groups, we will have to risk relationships both in the outside world and within the Christian community.

THE VERTICAL DIMENSION

No recommendations or prescriptions for the Christian future can bring improvement if they do not include strengthening the vertical dimension of our faith. God himself must be the focal point of our trust.

I have explored only two pressure points—renewal of apologetics and building true Christian community—out of many things that could be suggested for the renewal of the church. However true these points are in themselves, they will contribute nothing helpful if they are divorced from a deep conscious dependence on God alone.

Both the doing of apologetics and the building of community can be done as purely human activities, with no reference beyond the world of our own insights, resources, and capabilities. Nothing could be further from a biblical perspective.

One of the most challenging biblical insights into the nature of apologetics is found in Paul's second letter to the Corinthians. The apostle was reflecting on his own ministry:

> Indeed, we live as human beings, but we do not wage war according to human standards; for the weapons of our warfare are not merely human, but they have divine power to destroy strongholds. We destroy arguments and every proud obstacle raised up against the knowledge of God, and we take every thought captive to obey Christ (2 Corinthians 10:3–5).

Paul was writing about the battles of the Christian ministry being fought not with the tools of a normal army but with weapons that have God's power to destroy. What is surprising here is that he does not mention the things that we might first think of regarding spiritual warfare, such as prayer, fasting, or other directly spiritual activities. Certainly he does not want to exclude these things from the spiritual battle nor does he deem them unimportant. He simply wants to draw attention to a different issue at this point.

Paul emphasizes that warfare is fought by destroying arguments and whatever stands against knowledge of God in people's lives, and by submitting all our thinking to Christ's lordship. He speaks of this nonworldly war as a battle taking place over issues of truth in the minds and hearts of men and women.

The warfare is "destroying" in the sense that it disenchants, dissuades, and undeceives people in their trust of anything less than the true God. Positively, it builds confidence in the truth of Christ as applied to all areas of life. This is a battle of persuasion, of helping people to see through their illusions, and of building conviction in the truth and wonder of Jesus Christ.

This is part of the unseen battle where divine power is at work. As we try to understand our culture that we might better commend Christ in it, we are not doing a worldly intellectual exercise but the work of God. Therefore we need to draw on divine powers to equip us. If wrestling with this battle of persuasion in seriousness does not drive us to prayer, perhaps nothing will.

Just as our apologetics must be a deeply spiritual activity for which we pray for the power of God to work in and through us, likewise community building must be done in conscious dependence on God. These pressure points are not just "how to" strategies to remodel the social structure of the church. In fact we do not have a blueprint of what the church as community is meant to look like. The church needs individuals and groups to seek God in fresh ways and to know how to express their relationships with each other in the modern world.

Francis Schaeffer stated well the often forgotten vertical dimension of Christian community.

. . . regardless of its outward form, the Christian community as a community should understand that *its* first relationship is not horizontal, but vertical. The Christian community is made up of those who are in a personal relationship with God, and then the community *as a unit* is to strive to be first of all in a relationship with God. . . . The first thing the Christian community should do is to stand *as a community* in a living, existential, moment-by-moment relationship to God. [They] should stand in awe and worship waiting before God. . . .

Community relationship to God does not come mechanically. . . . It is something that must be consciously and continuously sought after. The individual, and then the group, must consciously look to Christ for help, consciously look to the leadership of the Holy Spirit not only theoretically but in reality, consciously understanding that every relationship must first be towards God before it has meaning out towards men. And only after the vertical relationship—first individually and then as a group—is established are we ready to have horizontal relationships and a proper Christian community. It is a long way to come. But there is no other way to achieve authenticity.[5]

Most Christians can understand what it is to look to God as individuals who seek strength and guidance. And we are used to doing it in families and small groups. But it seems as if the larger the group, the more difficult it becomes to continue seeking God's leadership. It seems much easier to operate under principles of the managerial or corporate world.

Notice in Schaeffer's quotation his repetition of the words "conscious" and "consciously." He was suggesting that radically trusting God as a group is an unnatural thing to do in our modern setting. It takes special, conscious intention.

A powerful biblical example reveals a group suddenly awakened to their need to take the vertical dimension of their community seriously. This was the Sanhedrin, the major ruling body of the Jewish nation in the early days of the Christian church.

The high priest had arrested and imprisoned the apostles for speaking of Jesus in public places. As they assembled the

Sanhedrin, a body of seventy men, they discovered that the apostles had already escaped from the jail and were preaching in the temple again. When some advised that they should be killed, Gamaliel, a respected scholar, rose and spoke. He pointed out that they had seen several false messiahs who created much excitement but who were killed and came to nothing.

He advised, "So in the present case, I tell you, keep away from these men and let them alone; because if this plan or this undertaking is of human origin, it will fail; but if it is of God, you will not be able to overthrow them—in that case you may even be found fighting against God!" (Acts 5:38–39)

Until Gamaliel spoke, the Sanhedrin's thinking had been dominated by purely practical and political concerns. The group seemed to be enclosed within the walls of their own personal ambitions and the interests of "national security." Gamaliel reminded them that God himself was a player in the story. If they paid attention to practical concerns alone, he said, they could easily find themselves in the position of fighting against God—a highly impractical situation. The community that claims to honor God must allow him his rightful position.

FOUNDATION FOR HOPE

With so many changes called for by the risen Christ and each of them so profound and far-reaching, how can we dare to hope that such change is possible? Or with the polarization between the chameleon and musk ox so deeply ingrained already, isn't it unrealistic to challenge it or expect anything to be different?

We can hope; it's not too late. In fact, the greater danger is to become resigned to a mediocrity that falls so far short of what Jesus has commanded. We should fear those voices who offer hope in an organized charge into the camp of either the chameleon or the musk ox.

And we are not alone. The Holy Spirit has begun to make his people restless; an enormous number of Christian people are frustrated by the way things are and want a better choice than between rigidity and conformity.

Our hope lies in being open to the challenge of the Bible into our individual and collective lives. God himself will guide us in ways that we could never anticipate. What we need is a spirit of humility and open-ended hunger to learn and grow.

John Stott has captured this spirit well: "Life is a pilgrimage of learning, a voyage of discovery, in which our mistaken views are corrected, our distorted notions adjusted, our shallow opinions deepened and some of our vast ignorance diminished."[6]

What Stott speaks of is a lifelong process in which the word of God is our primary teacher. We may well see the church in a crisis of authority and identity. But the church is the church of the risen Christ. Our lifetimes occupy a very small space on the timeline of his unfolding kingdom.

We began this book with a query. Given the crisis of moral authority in our culture, and given the Christian foundation that exists for a solution, why are those concerned not beating down a path to the door of the church of Jesus Christ? Although we have seen quite a number of reasons why this might be so, we have not given a blueprint for how the church will take more cultural leadership and be a major contributor to solving our society's problems. Instead, this book has been an appeal to the church to put our own house in order. As we return to the most basic teachings of Jesus himself, we will be able to honor him.

For he has made himself known to his churches saying, "Do not be afraid; I am the first and the last, and the living one. I was dead, and see, I am alive forever and ever; and I have the keys of Death and of Hades" (Revelation 1:17–18). Jesus' words are "the words of the holy one, the true one, who has the key of David, who opens and no one will shut, who shuts and no one opens" (Revelation 3:7). And so "let anyone who has an ear listen to what the Spirit is saying to the churches" (Revelation 3:22).

Appendix

FOLLOWING IS A LIST OF RESOURCES to explore further the apologetic issues we raised in chapter 4.

Modern Relativism

Carson, D.A. *The Gagging of God*. Grand Rapids, Mich.: Zondervan, 1996.

Heim, Mark. *Is Christ the Only Way?* Valley Forge, Pa.: Judson Press, 1985.

Netland, Harold. *Dissonant Voices*. Grand Rapids, Mich.: Eerdmans, 1991.

Newbigin, Lesslie. *The Gospel in a Pluralistic Society*. Grand Rapids, Mich.: Eerdmans and Geneva: WCC Publications, 1989.

Postmodern Suspicion

Lundin, Roger. *The Culture of Interpretation*. Grand Rapids, Mich.: Eerdmans, 1993.

Phillips, Timothy and Dennis L. Okholm. *Christian Apologetics in the Postmodern World*. Downers Grove, Ill.: InterVarsity Press, 1995.

Veith, Gene Edward. *Postmodern Times*. Wheaton, Ill.: Crossway Books, 1994.

The Implausibility of Transcendence

Berger, Peter L. *A Rumor of Angels*. New York: Doubleday, 1969.

Guinness, Os. *The Gravedigger File*. Downers Grove, Ill.: InterVarsity Press, 1983.

—————. *The Call*. Nashville, Tenn.: Word Publishing, 1998.

Loss of the Belief in Sin

Gilkey, Langdon. *Shantung Compound*. New York: Harper & Row, 1966.

Peters, Ted. *Sin, Radical Evil in Soul and Society*. Grand Rapids, Mich.: Eerdmans, 1994.

Plantinga, Cornelius. *Not the Way It's Supposed to Be*. Grand Rapids, Mich.: Eerdmans, 1995.

Charges against Christianity

Alexander, John. *The Secular Squeeze*. Downers Grove, Ill.: InterVarsity Press, 1993.

Brown, Ann. *An Apology to Women*. Downers Grove, Ill.: InterVarsity Press, 1991.

Chesterton, G. K. *Orthodoxy*. New York: Doubleday, 1990.

De Witt, Calvin, ed. *The Environment and the Christian*. Grand Rapids, Mich.: Baker Books, 1991.

Eberly, Don E. *Restoring the Good Society*. Grand Rapids, Mich.: Hourglass/Baker, 1993.

Gay, Craig M. *With Liberty and Justice for Whom?* Grand Rapids, Mich.: Eerdmans, 1991.

Guinness, Os. *The American Hour*. New York: Free Press, 1993.

Macaulay, Ranald and Jerram Barrs. *Being Human*. Downers Grove, Ill.: InterVarsity Press, 1978.

O'Connor, Flannery. *Mystery and Manners*. New York: Farrar, Straus & Giroux, 1969.

Schmidt, Thomas. *Straight and Narrow?* Downers Grove, Ill.: InterVarsity Press, 1995.

Veith, Gene Edward. *State of the Arts: From Bezalel to Mapplethorpe*. Wheaton, Ill.: Crossway, 1991.

Walls, Andrew. *The Missionary Movement in Christian History*. Maryknoll, N.Y.: Orbis Books, 1996.

Wilkinson, Loren, ed. *Earthkeeping in the Nineties*. Grand Rapids, Mich.: Eerdmans, 1991.

Notes

Chapter 1: The Power of Polarization

1. Walter Lippmann, *A Preface to Morals* (London: George Allen & Unwin, Ltd., 1931), p. 1.
2. Ibid., pp. 3–4.
3. Alzina Stone Dale, *Outline of Sanity* (Grand Rapids, Mich.: Eerdmans, 1983), p. 66.

Chapter 2: The Christian Chameleon

1. C. S. Lewis, "The Inner Ring," *The Weight of Glory* (Grand Rapids, Mich.: Eerdmans, 1979), pp. 55–66.
2. The whole of chapter 5 is devoted to exploring this question further.
3. J. D. Hunter, *Evangelicalism* (Chicago: University of Chicago Press, 1987), p. 20.
4. H. Nouwen, *The Wounded Healer* (New York: Image Books, Doubleday, 1972), pp. 86–87.
5. Robert Bellah, *Habits of the Heart* (New York: Harper & Row, 1985), pp. 45–48 and Francis A. Schaeffer, *How Shall We Then Live* (Old Tappan, N.J.: Fleming H. Revell, 1976), pp. 205 ff. Bellah uses the terms *therapist* and *manager*. Schaeffer's analysis was much the same ten years earlier, but he used the terminology of *personal peace* and *affluence*.
6. Hunter, *Evangelicalism*, p. 70.
7. Ibid.

8. J. D. Hunter, *American Evangelicalism* (New Brunswick, N.J.: Rutgers University Press, 1983), p. 81.
9. Ibid., p. 90.

Chapter 3: Tribal Life

1. My use of the word "tribal" should not be understood to mean something negative in itself. In fact, many tribal structures in premodern settings should be respected because they have positive elements that modern society has destroyed. My point is that the church as a church cannot be tribal if it is to be salt and light.
2. See George Marsden, *The Soul of the American University* (Oxford: Oxford University Press, 1992).
3. "Beer," *Consumer Reports*, July 1983, p. 342.
4. Matthew Henry, *Matthew Henry's Commentary on the Whole Bible*, vol. VI (New York: Fleming Revell), p. 977.
5. See Ephesians 5:21 and following.
6. Benjamin Barber, "Jihad vs McWorld," *Atlantic Monthly*, March 1992, p. 62.

Chapter 4: The Recovery of Apologetics

1. See 1 Peter 3:15.
2. See Acts 13:16–41; 17:2–3, 11.
3. See Acts 14:15–17; 17:22–31; 24:25.
4. Douglas Webster, "Evangelizing the Church," in *Christian Apologetics in the Postmodern World*, eds. Timothy R. Phillips & Dennis L. Okholm (Downers Grove, Ill.: InterVarsity Press, 1995), p. 195.
5. Frank Gannon, "Endpaper, Seeking Certitude," *New York Times Magazine*, 2 October 1994, p. 100.
6. John Kilner, "Culture War Casualties," *Christianity Today*, 6 March 1995, p. 26.

Chapter 5: One Truth, One Way

1. John Hick, *An Interpretation of Religion* (New Haven, Conn.: Yale University Press, 1989), p. 194.
2. Mark Heim, *Is Jesus the Only Way?* (Valley Forge, Pa.: Judson Press, 1985), p. 18.

3. C. S. Lewis, *Surprised by Joy* (San Diego: Harcourt, Brace & Jovanovich, 1955), p. 60.
4. Alan Watts, *Beyond Theology* (Cleveland, Ohio: Meridian Books, The World Publishing Co., 1968), pp. xi–xii.
5. Blaise Pascal, *Pensées*, ed. Louis Lafuma, trans. A. J. Krailheimer (New York: Penguin, 1966), p. 65, no. 131.

Chapter 6: The Church as Community

1. Robert Bellah, et al., *Habits of the Heart* (New York: Harper & Row, 1985), p. 72 ff.
2. Dietrich Bonhoeffer, *Life Together* (London: SCM Press, 1970), p. 15.
3. M. Scott Peck, *The Different Drum* (New York: Simon and Schuster, 1988), pp. 86–106.
4. Robert Reich, "Secession of the Successful," *New York Times Magazine*, 20 January 1991, p. 17.
5. See 1 Corinthians 12:12–31.
6. Francis Schaeffer, *The Church at the End of the Twentieth Century* (London: Norfolk Press, 1970), p. 46.
7. Tim Keller, unpublished paper, "How to Plant a Center City Church," 1997, p. 2.
8. See 1 Timothy 2:12–15 and 1 Corinthians 14:33–36.

Chapter 7: Returning to the Foundations

1. Lamin Sanneh, *Translating the Message* (Maryknoll, N.Y.: Orbis Books, 1990), p. 48.
2. See Numbers 22 and following.
3. See Numbers 31:16.
4. G. K. Chesterton, *The Everlasting Man* (New York: Doubleday, 1962), p. 245.
5. Francis A. Schaeffer, *The Church and the End of the Twentieth Century* (London: Norfolk Press, 1970), pp. 70–71.
6. James M. Gordon, *Evangelical Spirituality* (London: SPCK, 1991), p. 298.

DICK KEYES grew up in Massachusetts and studied history at Harvard University and theology at Westminster Theological Seminary. He and his wife, Mardi, have three sons and have worked with L'Abri Fellowship since 1970, first in Switzerland, then in England, and now at the L'Abri residential study center in Southborough, Massachusetts. While in England he served as a minister in the International Presbyterian Church in London for eight years.

His areas of particular interest include apologetics, the intersection between psychology and theology, and Christianity and culture. He is author of *True Heroism* (NavPress, 1995) and *Beyond Identity* (Servant, 1984; Paternoster, 1998).